D1375666

The UK Tax System:
an introduction

Second edition

Malcolm James

University of Wales Institute, Cardiff

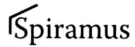

Spiramus

First published in 2005

This second edition published October 2009 by

Spiramus Press Ltd
102 Blandford Street
London W1U 8AG

www.spiramus.com

The right of Malcolm James to be identified as the author of this work has been asserted by him in accordance with the Copyright, Designs and Patents Act, 1988.

Disclaimer: This publication is intended to assist you in identifying issues which you should know about and about which you may need to seek specific advice. It is not intended to be an exhaustive statement of the law or a substitute for seeking specific advice. The contents of this book are intended to be general in nature and only provided for background information purposes. Neither this book nor any part of it constitutes, nor is a substitute for, legal advice which should still always be sought on any particular issue or in respect of any proposed activity or use and the author and publishers do not accept responsibility or liability for any loss or damage sustained by any person acting or placing reliance on the same or otherwise arising from its use.

© 2009 Spiramus Press Ltd

ISBN
Paperback   978 1904905 95 0
Hardback   978 1904905 96 7

Printed in Great Britain by the MPG Books Group, Bodmin and King's Lynn

Preface

I would to thank everyone at Spiramus Press for their assistance and comments in the writing of this book.

If anybody has comments for corrections or improvements to the book, please contact the publisher and I will be delighted to incorporate them into future editions.

The book reflects the law as at 31 July 2009.

For convenience the masculine pronoun has been used throughout and no discrimination is intended.

About the author

Malcolm James is a Senior Lecturer in Accounting and Taxation at the University of Wales Institute, Cardiff and has lectured widely on the subject of taxation on both professional and undergraduate courses. He has also lectured for the Chartered Institute of Taxation and written a number of articles for their journal *Tax Adviser*. He has also contributed regularly to CCH and Lexis Nexis tax publications. Before becoming a lecturer he worked for several large firms of accountants and also in industry.

Tables of authorities

Cases

Statutes

INTRODUCTION TO THE UK TAX SYSTEM

Contents

Chapter 1. The Legal Framework of Taxation

1.1. Sources of Tax Legislation and Practice

The main sources of taxation law and practice in the UK are:
- statute law;
- extra-statutory concessions (ESCs);
- other HM Revenue & Customs (HMRC) concessions;
- Statutory Instruments (SIs);
- Statements of Practice (SPs);
- Press Releases;
- European directives and regulations;
- case law;
- HM Revenue & Customs (HMRC) guidance manuals.

1.2. Statute Law

1.2.1. Taxes Acts

Statute is a major, but by no means dominant, part of UK taxation law and consists of the following major acts:
- Income and Corporation Taxes Act 1988 *(ICTA 1988)*;
- Income Tax (Earnings and Pensions Act) 2003 *(ITEPA 2003)*;
- Income Tax (Trading and Other Income) Act 2005 *(ITTOIA 2005)*;
- Income Tax Act 2007 *(ITA 2007)*;
- Corporation Tax Act 2009 *(CTA 2009)*;
- Capital Allowances Act 2001 *(CAA 2001)*;
- Taxation of Capital Gains Act 1992 *(TCGA 1992)*;
- Value Added Tax Act 1994 *(VATA 1994)*;
- Inheritance Tax Act 1984 *(IHTA 1984)*;
- Social Security Contributions and Benefits Act 1992 *(SSCBA 1992)*;
- Taxes Management Act 1970 *(TMA 1970)*;
- Customs and Excise Management Act 1979 *(CEMA 1979)*.
- Finance Acts.

Each year the Finance Act may add new sections to these acts and amend and repeal others, so that after a number of years the numbering of the various acts has become somewhat confusing. Periodically an act and the subsequent amendments are therefore consolidated into a new act. Consolidating acts are merely the re-arrangement of existing legislation into a single act, with a logical numbering of sections, and do not amend the legislation. For example, before 2001 the main act on capital allowances was the Capital Allowances Act 1990, so that *CAA 2001* was a consolidation of the earlier act and amendments enacted between 1990 and 2000. It was also the first act to be written in simpler

English as part of the Tax Law Rewrite project, in which the language in which the legislation was expressed (although not the legislation itself) was simplified. As part of consolidation and re-writing ICTA 1988 is being split into a number of different acts, the first four of which are ITEPA 2003, ITTOIA 2005, ITA 2007, and CTA 2009. CTA 2009 by no means includes all corporation tax legislation and significant portions of the legislation, such as that relating to losses, groups and close companies, remain in ICTA 1988. These will be incorporated into a second Corporation Tax Act.

1.2.2. The Legislative Process

The passage of a Finance Act starts with the Budget delivered by the Chancellor of the Exchequer, usually in March, although from 1993 to 1996 the Budget was held in November to coincide with the annual spending review. Approximately two weeks after the Budget the Finance Act is published and passes through the following stages before receiving royal assent:

1. *First reading*
   This is a formality at which a dummy of the bill is laid before the House and its title is read out. It is ordered to be printed and a date for a second reading is fixed.

2. *Second reading*
   The legislation is debated in detail. Some of the clauses relating to the imposition of tax rather than technical matters are sent to a committee of the whole House for further debate. The remainder of the bill is sent to a Standing Committee of between 16 and 50 MPs.

3. *Committee stage*
   The bill is discussed in detail, clause by clause and schedule by schedule, and amendments are proposed by both the Government and the Opposition. Amendments may either be agreed upon, withdrawn, or a vote may be forced.

4. *Report stage*
   The amended bill is reported back to the full House. Further amendments and additions may be made at this stage.

5. *Third reading*
   This is a brief debate on the bill as a whole.

6. *House of Lords*
   The bill is debated very briefly in the House of Lords, but they have no power to make amendments to bills relating to public taxation.

An act comes into force on the day that it receives royal assent, or on another day specified in the act. In the case of the Finance Act provisions generally come into force on Budget Day or at the start of the tax year.

The Finance Act must receive royal assent by 5 August.

1.2.3. Provisional Collection of Tax

Provisions contained in the Budget come into force on Budget Day or the start of the following tax year, or on another date specified by Ministers, whereas the Finance Act does not usually receive royal assent until July. In order to collect taxes in the intervening period a resolution must be passed under the Provisional Collection of Taxes Act 1968 stating that it is 'expedient in the public interest' to introduce, abolish or vary a tax'. This resolution must be followed by a confirmatory resolution within the following ten parliamentary business days and comes into effect if, within 30 parliamentary business days of the original resolution, either the Finance Bill containing the provisions set out in the resolution receives its second reading or the provisions are inserted into the Finance Bill as an amendment at the committee stage.

A resolution ceases to have effect if:
- the Finance Act is passed;
- the provisions contained in the resolution are rejected;
- Parliament is dissolved or prorogued.

Where a resolution ceases to have effect, is amended, or a provisional resolution is not followed within ten days by a confirmatory resolution, or the confirmatory resolution amends the provisional resolution, any tax collected under the provisional resolution must be repaid or adjusted.

1.3. Secondary Sources of Tax Legislation and Practice

1.3.1. HM Revenue & Customs Concessions

Although parliamentary draftsmen make every effort to ensure that the law will operate as intended, there are sometimes areas at the margins where this is not the case and certain taxpayers may be unfairly disadvantaged. If it is considered that the scale of the problem does not merit the time and expense of amending the legislation, HM Revenue & Customs will issue a statement known as an Extra-statutory Concession, stating that in certain circumstances they will observe the spirit rather than the strict letter of the law. Since these are in writing, a taxpayer can rely on them, unless he seeks to use them for the purpose of tax avoidance, in which case HMRC will interpret the law strictly.

Not all HM Revenue & Customs concessions are in writing. There are various informal concessions, some of which are well-known and are universally applied throughout HMRC, and others which may have been agreed between an individual taxpayer, or his advisors, and the Officers responsible for his tax affairs. These concessions have generally been made for reasons of administrative convenience rather than because the legislation operates inequitably. These practices and concessions are mostly unwritten, although recently HMRC have issued some of these in writing.

1.3.2. Statutory Instruments

Statutory Instruments are documents setting out detailed regulations relating to an area of tax. These are laid before parliament and automatically become law after 40 days, unless objections are raised. Statutory Instruments may also be used to introduce legislation where parliamentary time is short or particular expertise is necessary.

1.3.3. Statements of Practice

Despite the provisions of the various statutes and the decisions of the courts, there are still areas of taxation which remain unclear. HM Revenue & Customs have issued a number of Statements of Practice, which state their interpretation of the law and which aim, among other things, to ensure consistency between different tax offices. These statements do not have the force of law and HMRC reserve the right to argue for a different tax treatment if the facts of the case so dictate. Equally, the taxpayer may argue that a different interpretation is appropriate in certain circumstances and may challenge the legal validity of the practice. Since the inception of the Taxpayers' Charter, HM Revenue & Customs may be more reluctant to depart from a Statement of Practice.

1.3.4. Press Releases

Press Releases are the means by which HM Revenue & Customs communicate changes in the law or practice to the taxpayer and tax advisors. Extra-statutory Concessions, Statements of Practice and the Chancellor's Budget proposals are all first announced in Press Releases.

1.3.5. Internal Revenue & Customs Guidance Manuals

HM Revenue & Customs produce guidance manuals for the use of their Officers to ensure that they apply the law in a consistent manner and make appropriate enquiries. In recent years these have been published for use by practitioners, although certain sections still remain confidential. The manuals set out HM Revenue & Customs' interpretation of the law, and in contentious areas, this may not coincide with the view of tax practitioners. The advice given in these manuals should therefore be read in a critical spirit and not always taken as definitive.

1.4.   European Sources

Since the UK joined the EU in 1973, the UK has been subject to legislation originating from the EU. European law prevails in the case of a conflict with UK law. European legislation is of four types:

1. *Treaties*
    These rank as primary legislation within the EU.

2. *Directives*
    These do not take effect directly but must be incorporated into the domestic legislation of a member state, although they may have effect even if they have not been incorporated into domestic law, provided that they are sufficiently precise, unambiguous and unconditional.

3. *Regulations*
    These take effect in member states directly, without legislation being passed by the individual parliaments.

4. *Decisions*
    These are addressed to individual states and are binding only on that state.

Directives, regulations and decisions are classified as secondary legislation.

UK tax law has also been affected by judgments by the European Court of Justice. For example, the Finance Act 2000 amended the group relief rules (the surrender of trading and other losses to other companies in the same group), after the European Court of Justice had ruled that the existing rules breached European law. In 2005 the Court heard another case brought by Marks and Spencer concerning the legality of the UK group relief provisions, who claimed that a refusal by HM Revenue & Customs to allow it to offset a trading loss of a French subsidiary against the profits of the UK parent breached European law. If it had succeeded the case would have had far-reaching implications for group relief in the UK, and in other EU countries. The preliminary judgment indicates that it has only won a partial victory and, in this case, relatively little change needs to be made to UK law to make it compatible with European law. At one time the European Court of Justice largely restricted its judgments to the area of VAT. However, recently the court has increasingly turned its attention to the area of direct taxation, and, in particular, company taxation.

The method of interpretation of EU legislation tends to be rather different from the interpretation of UK legislation, since continental lawyers tend to take a more 'broad-brush' approach to interpreting an act, whereas UK lawyers tend to dissect an act word-for-word and line-by-line in order to discern its meaning. EU legislation tends also to be interpreted in the context of the aims of the EU as a whole, and legislation is often preceded by a preamble which explains the reasons for its enactment. The phrases contained within it are often vague, with the interpretation being left to judges.

1.5.   Case Law

1.5.1.   Introduction

There are significant areas of taxation, such as the distinction between capital and revenue expenditure, where statute provides very little guidance. For guidance on such points we must look to case law. Even where an area of taxation is covered by statute there may be areas of dispute which must be resolved by the courts. In cases of a dispute the taxpayer may appeal in the first instance to a First-tier tribunal and an appeal against the decision of the tribunal may be made to the Upper Tribunal, followed by the Appeal Court and finally the Supreme Court, which is the ultimate authority in the UK.[1] (Before March 2009 the sequence went: Special Commissioners to High Court, Appeal Court and then the House of Lords.) The objective of the courts is to ascertain the meaning of the statute, therefore words contained in statute must be given their ordinary meaning, although this has at times led to an absurd result *(IRC v Hinchy (1960) (38 TC 625))*. A contrary approach followed in *Mangin v IRC (1971) (AC 739)* has been to give words their normal meaning, but to assume that no injustice or absurdity was intended. An interpretation may also depart from the literal interpretation where words are ambiguous or ambivalent, in which case the interpretation most favourable to the taxpayer will be adopted. It may not, however, correct an error in the wording of an act, where the wording does not give rise to the effect intended. Where legislation is ambiguous it is possible to refer to ministerial statements as reported in Hansard to ascertain the intended meaning of an act.

1.6.   Classifications of Income

Historically, income was divided into a number of schedules, some of which were sub-divided into a number of cases. Thus income from property in the UK was designated as Schedule A income and the profits of a trade were designated as Schedule D Case I income. Various schedules were abolished over the years and the system was finally abolished for income tax by ITTOIA

---

[1] This is with effect from October 2009.

2005 and for corporation tax by CTA 2009. Income in a return is now simply referred to by a descriptive name, such as trading income or employment income.

1.7. Tax Years and Financial Years

Income tax is assessed by reference to a tax year, which ends on 5 April and is described by referring to the two calendar years which it straddles. The year ending on 5 April 2010 is therefore the tax year 2009/10. The origin of this distinctly eccentric year end is that until the mid 18th century the tax year ended on 25 March, which was one of the four traditional quarter days (and the start of the church, being the feast of the Annunciation nine months before Christmas). In 1752 the Government adopted the Gregorian calendar, as a result of which 11 days (3-13 September) were lost and, since they were unwilling for the tax year to last only 354 days, the end of the tax year was moved back to 5 April.

Corporation tax was introduced in 1965 and companies are assessed by reference to a financial year, which ends on 31 March and is referred to by the calendar year in which it commences. The financial year ending on 31 March 2010 is, therefore, termed the financial year 2009 (abbreviated to FY09). As a result, legislation introduced in the Finance Act will often come into force on 1 April for companies, but on 6 April for individuals.

Chapter 2. Income Tax Computation

2.1.   Aggregation of Taxpayer's Income

A taxpayer's income from all sources must be aggregated in the tax computation, although each type of income should be shown separately (see comprehensive example chapter section 2.8). The income must be analysed between:

1. Non-savings income. The main types of income which fall into this category are trading profits, employment income and property income;

2. Savings income, other than dividends. Individuals receive bank and building society net of tax at 20%. The gross amount of the income is always entered in the computation and any income received net of tax must be grossed up 100/80. Some types of interest, such as interest from the National Savings Bank and interest on loans between individuals are received gross;

3. Dividends received from UK companies. These carry a tax credit of 10/90 of the net dividend. The dividend must therefore be grossed up by 100/90 in the tax computation. The tax credit is deducted from the taxpayer's liability, therefore where dividends fall within the starting and basic rate bands, there will be no additional liability. The tax credit is not repaid if there is no tax liability.

2.2.   Interest

Interest on the following categories of loans (which is paid gross) qualifies for tax relief and is deducted from total income:
- loan to purchase plant and machinery used in the business by a partner or employee;
- loan to purchase interest in a close company;
- loan to purchase interest in an employee-controlled company;
- loan to purchase an interest in a partnership or to contribute to partnership capital; and
- investment in a co-operative.

If only part of a loan is used for a qualifying purpose, a deduction may only be claimed for the interest on the portion of the loan used for a qualifying purpose.

2.3.   Payments to Charities

Any gift of money to a registered charity qualifies for relief, provided that:
- it is not subject to any condition of repayment;

- the payment does not fall within the payroll deduction scheme and is not deductible in calculating the individual's income from any specific source;
- the payment is not conditional on, associated with, or part of any arrangement involving the acquisition of property by the charity from the individual; and
- a gift aid declaration is made.

The payment must be a gift and the payer must not receive valuable consideration in return. There are, however, a couple of exceptions:

- free or reduced entry to properties preserved, maintained, kept or created by a charity for its charitable purposes is permitted, provided that *either* the public can obtain admission at all times during a 12-month period or the gift is at least 10% greater than the admission price granting similar rights that would otherwise be payable. A subscription to the National Trust will therefore fall within the gift aid scheme.

- the value of any benefits obtained in return is ignored if they do not exceed the following amounts.

Amount of Gross Donation	Permissible Benefit
£1 - £100	25%
£101 - £1,000	£25
£1,001 or more	2.5%

- the total value of the benefits associated with the gift and any other qualifying gifts in the tax year must not exceed £500.

Relief for gifts to charities is given through the extension of the basic rate band (see example at end of chapter).

Relief is also available under certain circumstances where land and buildings or shares are gifted to a charity.

2.4.   Personal Allowances Deducted from Net Income

There are two types of personal allowances, namely those deducted from a taxpayer's net income and tax reducers (see section 2.6), although tax reducers are now of much less significance since they were largely abolished from 2000/01 onwards. There are three types of personal allowances which are deducted from the net income to arrive at a taxpayer's taxable income.

1.   Personal Allowance;
2.   Age Allowance;
3.   Blind Person's Allowance.

2.4.1. Personal Allowance (2009/10 £6,475)

This allowance is available to a taxpayer, including children, unless he qualifies for the increased age allowance. There are no provisions for carrying the personal allowance forward or back or transferring it between taxpayers. If it cannot be used in the tax year, it is lost.

2.4.2. Age Allowance (2009/10 £9,490)

The age allowance is first available in the tax year in which the taxpayer celebrates his 65th birthday. An increased age allowance (2009/10 £9,640) is available in the tax year in which the taxpayer celebrates his 75th birthday.

The full age allowance is only available to taxpayers whose adjusted net income does not exceed a threshold level (2009/10 £22,900). If the adjusted net income exceeds this threshold the age allowance is reduced by half of the excess until the allowance reaches the level of the standard Personal Allowance.

A taxpayer is entitled to the appropriate age allowance if he dies in the tax year of his 65th or 75th birthday, regardless of whether he dies before or after his birthday.

2.4.3. Blind Person's Allowance (2009/10 £1,890)

This allowance is given to a taxpayer who is registered blind. When a taxpayer first claims the allowance, he may also claim it for the previous tax year provided that he can show that he was also blind in that tax year.

2.5. Computation of Tax

There are three different sets of tax rates, one for non-savings income, one for savings income and one for dividend income. These are:

	Non-savings income	Savings income	Dividends
Starting rate £2,440	20%	10%	10%
Basic rate (next £34,960)	20%	20%	10%
Higher rate (excess over £37,400)	40%	40%	32.5%

The bands are allocated to the categories of income in the following order:
- non-savings income;
- savings income;
- dividends.

The basic rate band is extended by the grossed up amount of charitable gift aid donations and pension contribution. Therefore a charitable donation of £400 will lead to an extension of the basic rate band by £500 (£400 x 100/80) to £37,900.

2.6.   Tax Reducers

2.6.1.   Categories of Tax Reducers

The following allowances may reduce the tax liability calculated in the previous stage, but can only reduce a tax liability to nil and cannot give rise to a repayment. The main types of tax reducers are:

- investment in Venture Capital Trusts (VCT);
- investment in Enterprise Investment Scheme (EIS) made before 6 April 2007;
- Qualifying maintenance payments;
- Married Couples' Age Allowance (including civil partners);
- Double tax relief – treaty relief;
- Double tax relief – unilateral relief.

Investments in VCTs give a tax reduction of 30%. EISs give a tax reduction at 20%, the others at 10%, e.g. the married couple's age allowance where the older spouse is between 65 and 74 is £6,965 and this translates into a tax reduction of £697.

The Married Couples' Age Allowance is only available where the older spouse, or in the case of civil partners in partnerships registered on or after 5 December 2005, the older partner was born before 6 April 1935.

2.6.2.   Reduction in MCAA

The MCAA may be restricted where the age allowance has been reduced to the level of the standard personal allowance. In this case any excess which could not be deducted from the age allowance is deducted from the MCAA. The MCAA cannot, however, fall below £2,670 (this is a notional figure which equates to the married couples' allowance which would have been available to married taxpayers in general if the allowance had not been abolished except for older couples). No restriction is made on account of the adjusted net income of the wife, however high that may be.

2.6.3.   Transfer of MCAA

The MCAA is given to the husband in the first instance, but his wife can make a unilateral election to receive £1,335 of the MCAA, i.e. half of the notional MCAA which would have available to all married taxpayers. A joint election may be made for his wife to receive £2,670 of the MCAA. Where either spouse has insufficient income to use the MCAA in full, any unused portion may be transferred to the other spouse by making an election by 31 January in the sixth year after the end of the tax year concerned.

2.6.4. Maintenance Payments

Maintenance payments only qualify for tax relief if the taxpayer was born before 6 April 1935. Relief is given at 10% on the lower of £2,670 and payments made in the tax year. The payments must be made to the ex-spouse or partner and not directly to the child. By concession, relief will be available where school fees are paid direct to the school.

2.7. Tax Retained on Interest, Royalties and Gift Aid Donations

In addition to tax on his own income, the taxpayer is also liable to pay tax retained on payments made net of tax. In doing this the taxpayer is acting as a tax collector for HM Revenue & Customs, and is paying the payee's basic rate liability on the income in the same way as a bank or building society acts as a tax collector for the investors' tax liability on interest. A taxpayer is obliged to pay over the tax retained, even if his income, ignoring the payment, would be less than his personal allowance and, therefore, the payment has not given him any tax reduction.

Where a taxpayer makes a gift aid donation, but does not pay tax at the basic rate on his income and/or his capital gains, the following allowances will be restricted to ensure that the tax retained on the donation is collected.

If this still does not achieve the right result, e.g. a taxpayer has no income or capital gains during a tax year, an assessment will be raised.

2.8. Comprehensive Example

Mr Jones, aged 43, has the following income in 2009/10:

Income Tax Computation

	Non-savings income	Non-dividend income	Dividends	Total	Tax suffered/ (withheld)
	£	£	£	£	
Trading income	37,220			37,220	
Rental income	4,500			4,500	
Building Society Interest £1,200 x 100/80		1,500		1,500	300
Dividends £2,700 x 100/90	_____	_____	3,000	3,000	300
Total income	41,720	1,500	3,000	46,220	£600
Interest	(600)	_____	_____	(600)	
Net income	41,120	1,500	3,000	45,620	
Personal Allowance	(6,475)	_____	_____	(6,475)	
Taxable Income	£34,645	£1,500	£3,000	£39,145	

Mr Jones also made gift aid donations totalling £400 (net) during 2009/10.

Mr Jones' basic rate band will be extended to:

	£
Basic rate band	37,400
Gift aid donations £400 x 100/80	500
	£37,900

Tax Payable

Non-savings Income	£
£34,645 @ 20%	6,929
Savings income	
£1,500 @ 20%	300
Dividends	
£1,755 @ 10%	175
£1,245 @ 32.5%	404
Tax Liability	7,808
Less: Tax Suffered	(600)
Tax payable	£7,208

2.9. Tax-free Sources of Income

The following are the most important tax-free sources of income:

- Interest from investments in Individual Savings Accounts (ISAs);
- lump sum payments from approved pension schemes;
- gifts;
- premium bond prizes, betting and lottery prizes and other competition winnings;
- some (but not all) social security benefits; and
- statutory redundancy pay up and certain other payments up on redundancy or dismissal up to a maximum of £30,000.

2.10. Death and Separation

2.10.1. Death

A taxpayer will receive any allowances to which he is entitled in full, even if he dies during the tax year.

2.10.2. Divorce and Separation

For tax purposes the relevant date is the date of separation rather than the date of divorce (or dissolution of a civil partnership). This will be the date of the court deed of separation or the date the couple separate in circumstances which are likely to be permanent. This does not necessarily mean that the couple are living under separate roofs. Spouses or civil partners are treated as single people from the date of separation, but in the tax year of separation the husband, or the civil partner receiving the MCAA will still receive the MCAA (if appropriate) and half or all of the minimum MCAA may be transferred to his wife or other civil partner.

Where a couple separate in one tax year and are reconciled in a later tax year, in the tax year of reconciliation the husband or civil partner will receive the full MCAA (if appropriate), whenever the reconciliation takes place in the tax year. If a couple are separated and reconciled within the same tax year the separation is ignored.

2.11. Married Couples – Joint Property

Where a married couple jointly own an income-bearing asset such as property or shares, HM Revenue & Customs will normally assume that they own equal shares and apportion half the income to each partner. This does not apply to certain types of income, the most important being partnership income and income from furnished holiday letting. A couple may, however, elect for the income to be apportioned in some other manner and this is a means by which a non-working spouse may use his personal allowance.

Any election must, however, reflect the facts and if one spouse wishes to transfer some or all of the income to the other spouse he must make an outright and irrevocable gift of the underlying asset. For example, where an attempt is made to transfer dividend income to the other spouse whilst retaining ownership of the underlying capital, HMRC will invoke anti-avoidance settlement rules.

2.12. Minor Children

Minor children are taxable persons and are entitled to a personal allowance, but most children simply do not have sufficient income to pay any tax.

Any income which has arisen from capital gifted from a child's parents is taxable on the parents. This, however, does not apply if:
- the amount of income arising in the tax year does not exceed £100, which covers items such as birthday and Christmas gifts;
- the child is employed in the parent's trade and the payment represents reasonable remuneration.

These provisions do not cover gifts by other family members such as grandparents, and the gifting of capital by grandparents directly to grandchildren is a common and effective tax planning strategy.

Chapter 3. Principles of Trading Income

3.1. Introduction

By definition, only income of a trading nature is assessable under this heading. It is therefore necessary first to ascertain whether a taxpayer is trading, and if he is held to be trading, to distinguish trading income from:

- income of a capital nature;
- income arising otherwise than from the trade;
- income received as an employee of a business rather than as a self-employed sub-contractor.

Similarly, in order for an expense to be deductible from trading profits, it must be:

- revenue, as opposed to capital, in nature. There are a number of exceptions where expenditure of a capital nature is expressly deductible by statute;
- incurred in the course of the business i.e. it is a proper debit under the principles of commercial accounting;
- not otherwise disallowed by statute.

Accounts should be drawn up so as to show a 'true and fair view' and in accordance with GAAP and, in general, the taxation treatment will follow the accounting treatment

3.2. Definitions of Trading

The legislation unfortunately gives very little guidance as to whether a particular activity constitutes trading. The definition states that a trade 'includes any venture in the nature of a trade', which merely means that whether an activity is a trade depends on the substance of what is being carried on and how it is being carried on, rather than the description given to it by an individual, and does not necessarily need to have all the attributes associated with a trade in order to be chargeable. It has therefore fallen to case law to provide more specific guidance, known as the badges of trade.

The tests are:

- whether an asset is held as an investment or for personal enjoyment. If so, any profit on sale is unlikely to be treated as a trading profit;
- whether there is a profit motive in the transaction;
- whether the subject matter of the transaction indicates;
- frequency of transactions. Trading, by its nature, generally involves frequent transactions;

- length of ownership. If goods are being traded, the trader would normally only own them for a short period;
- performing supplementary work on goods;
- manner in which assets are ccquired and circumstances surrounding sale. When goods are being traded the purchase and sale of these goods are deliberate acts.

3.3.   Capital and Revenue Receipts.

3.3.1.   Treatment of Transactions

General Principles

In general the taxation treatment of transactions will follow the accounting treatment i.e. if a receipt or expense is included in the profit and loss account of a business, it will be treated as a revenue item and if it is treated as a capital receipt in the accounts it will be so treated for taxation purposes. The accounting treatment is, however, not conclusive. Whilst the great majority of receipts and payments will clearly fall into one or other of these categories, the distinction will sometimes be an extremely fine one.   For example, compensation received will normally be treated as a trading receipt on the grounds that it replaces lost trading profits, but in *Glenboig Union Fireclay Co v IRC (1921) (12 TC 427 HL)*, compensation received by the company in return for agreeing not to work a bed of fireclay which it owned under a railway was held to be capital on the grounds that it compensated for the permanent loss or sterilisation of a traders' profit-making apparatus.

3.3.2.   Non-contractual Receipts

Where a trader receives an amount which the payer has no contractual obligation to make, it will not be taxable provided:

- the payment is unsolicited;
- any business connection has ceased before the payment is made;
- the payment is not for past services and there should be no suggestion that fees charged by the recipient in the past were less than the market rate;
- the payment is not an advance payment or retainer for future services;
- the payment is not compensation for loss of business.

3.3.3.   Deductions from Trading Profits

Expenditure may be deducted from trading profits if it is revenue in nature and is wholly and exclusively for business purposes. The question of whether a payment is revenue or capital will largely follow the accounting treatment, although the courts have formulated the following tests, notwithstanding the accounting treatment:

- Expenditure on fixed capital i.e. assets such as factory machinery which are held for the long term in order that they may generate profit, will be capital expenditure;
- Expenditure on circulating capital i.e. assets such as trading stock which will be sold in the short term in order to generate profit, will be revenue expenditure;
- Where expenditure brings about an enduring benefit, often by bringing a new asset into existence, the expenditure will generally be considered to be capital. An initial payment made by the company to set up a pension fund was ruled to be capital. Subsequent annual payments into the pension fund were, however, treated as revenue, since they were merely maintaining an existing asset.

In order to be deductible, expenditure must not be remote from the trade. For example, although the annual costs of preparing a tax return are deductible, the costs of filing a tax appeal are not deductible since they arise in an individual's capacity as a taxpayer rather than as a trader. Similarly, a loss due to fraud by a director is not deductible, since it is not considered to be business-related, although a loss due to fraud by a junior employee is considered to be a normal business risk and is deductible.

Some types of expense can have a dual purpose, part of the expenditure being attributable to trading and part being private expenditure:
- a businessman who makes calls from his home may deduct the cost of business calls, but it is not possible to apportion the line rental charge, which is disallowable;
- if a car is used for both business and private motoring, the business motoring expenses will be deductible. It is necessary to keep a record of business and private motoring to support the apportionment;
- where part of a trader's residence is used as an office, an appropriate proportion of household expenses such as heating and mortgage interest will be deductible, but the trader should be aware that principal private residence relief will not be available on this proportion of any gain on the disposal of the property.

Sometimes expenditure will have a dual purpose, but is not capable of being analysed between business and private use and in this case the expenditure is not deductible. For example, it is not possible, in general, to claim a deduction for the cost of business clothing. The courts have held that clothing is necessary for warmth and decency and that this element cannot be separated from the need to portray a suitable, professional image *(Mallalieu v Drummond (1983) (2 AC 386, BTC 380))*. This principle is, however, not taken to unreasonable lengths and the cost of specialist clothing, e.g. protective clothing or a clown's outfit, will be deductible.

3.4. Deductible Expenditure –a Summary

The following table gives a summary of the tax treatment of the major items of expenditure commonly incurred by businesses.

Depreciation and profit or loss on disposal of fixed assets	Disallowable – relief obtained through capital allowances.
Wages and salaries	Allowable, provided not excessive for duties performed. Otherwise only appropriate amount deductible.
Provisions and write-offs, e.g. bad debts	Deductible, provided provision complies with FRS12. Increases in general provisions are not deductible and decreases not assessable. Write-offs and provisions of non-business nature not deductible.
Subscriptions	Allowable, provided business in nature
Donations	Allowable if for purpose of trade, e.g. to trade benevolent association, or if small donation is made to local organisation.
Legal & professional fees	Allowable, provided incurred on item which is business related and revenue in nature.
Entertainment	Disallowable, except for expenditure on entertainment of employees.
Gifts	Allowable, if trader's name is clearly shown on item, gifts of no more than £50 p.a. are made to same person and gift is not food, alcohol or tobacco.
Samples	Allowable
Appropriations of profit	Disallowable. Appropriations of goods must be credited at selling price rather than cost price.
Repairs and maintenance	Allowable, provided that expenditure

	simply returns assets to original state and any element of improvement is simply due to advances in technology.
Fines	Disallowable, except for parking fines of employees incurred whilst on business, if these payments constitute earnings in the hands of the employee.
Interest and bank charges	Allowable, provided incurred for business purposes.
Pre-trading expenditure	Allowable, provided expenditure incurred in seven years prior to commencement of trading and would otherwise be deductible.

3.5. Capital Allowances

3.5.1. Definitions

Capital allowances are a replacement for depreciation charged in the accounts and may be claimed on plant and machinery. The definition of plant and machinery for this purpose is far wider than might be expected, and includes assets for permanent use in carrying on the business and which are not part of the setting in which the trade is carried on. This means that the asset must perform a function in the context of the particular trade. Normal lighting is therefore part of the building, whereas specialised lighting such as lighting in display windows and spotlights for diamond cutting have a specific function in the trade, and qualify for capital allowances. Doors in a warehouse which simply grant normal access do not qualify for capital allowances, whereas electrically operated roller doors, which specifically allow for vehicles such as fork-lift trucks to move about the warehouse easily, do qualify. It has also been held in the case of *IRC v Scottish and Newcastle Breweries Ltd (1982) (55 TC 252)* that part of the trade of hotelier and innkeeper consisted of providing 'atmosphere' or 'ambience', and that wall decor such as pictures, murals, tapestries and other items which contribute to the creation of an appropriate atmosphere perform a function in this context, rather than merely being a part of the setting.

3.5.2. Allowances

A writing down allowance may be claimed on expenditure not previously written off. The expenditure not written off is known as the tax written down value. This allowance was reduced from 25% to 20% for accounting periods of 12 months with effect from 1 April 2008 for companies and from 6 April 2008 for unincorporated businesses.

In addition an annual investment allowance allows the first £50,000 of expenditure in a period to be written off in full.

A first year allowance was available to small and medium-sized businesses for a number of years, but was abolished with effect from 6 April 2008 for unincorporated businesses and 1 April 2008 for companies and was replaced by the annual investment allowance. However, FA 2009 has, as a temporary measure, re-introduced these, allowing 40% of expenditure incurred in 2009/10 (FY09 for companies) in excess of the annual investment allowance to be written off. A writing down allowance may not be claimed on expenditure in a tax year if a first year allowance is being claimed. Certain items of plant, such as cars with an emissions' rating of 110g/km or less, qualify for a 100% first year allowance, i.e. they are effectively treated as revenue expenditure in the year of acquisition.

Certain items are termed **special rate** expenditure, such as thermal insulation and cars with an emissions' rating of over 160g/km or more, and a writing down allowance of 10% p.a. may be claimed on such expenditure. No annual investment allowance or first year allowance may be claimed.

3.5.3. Pooling of Plant and Machinery
Most items of plant and machinery are pooled in either the general pool or the special rate pool, i.e. the expenditure is simply added to a single total and the different items lose their identity. The following items are not included in a pool:
- cars acquired on or before 5 April 2009 (31 March 2009 for companies) costing over £12,000. The writing down allowance on these cars is restricted to a maximum of £3,000. Vehicles other than cars, such as lorries, may be included in the general pool an annual investment allowance or first year allowance may be claimed as appropriate.
- assets with an element of private use. These will usually, but need not, be vehicles.

3.5.4. Disposals
Where an asset in the general pool is disposed of, the lower of cost and sale proceeds (in practice this will almost always be the sale proceeds), is deducted from the pool balance. Where an asset which is not included in a pool is disposed of, the lower of cost and sale proceeds is deducted from the balance of expenditure not written off. Any excess of expenditure not written off over

the disposal value may be claimed in the year of disposal (balancing allowance). If the disposal value exceeds the expenditure not written off, this excess is deducted from capital allowances claimed (balancing charge).

3.5.5. Industrial Buildings Allowance

For many years an allowance of 4% of cost could be claimed on industrial buildings. This is now being gradually phased out and the allowance which may be claimed in 2009/10 is 2% of cost and the allowance will cease to be available from 2011/12 onwards.

3.6. Basis Periods

Because individuals are taxed by reference to a tax year and accounting periods are unlikely to coincide with the tax year, accounting periods must be matched with tax years. The profits assessed in a tax year are therefore those of the accounting period ending in the tax year. The accounting periods y/e 30 June 2009, 31 December 2009 or 31 March 2010 will therefore all be assessed in 2009/10 and are termed the basis period for the tax year. There are special rules for the opening and closing years of the business and when a trader changes his accounting date.

3.7. Losses

Loss-making periods are subject to the same rules concerning adjustments, capital allowances and basis periods, except that the end result is a loss rather than a profit. The assessment for the tax year is £NIL and a means has to be found of relieving the loss. The two main means of loss relief are:

- the loss is carried forward and offset against the next available trading profit from the same trade. If a loss of £8,000 is made in the year ended 31 December 2009, the basis period for 2009/10, it may be offset against any trading profits arising in 2010/11 with any remaining loss carried forward to 2011/12 etc;
- the loss may be offset against the taxpayer's total income of either the tax year of the loss or the preceding tax year. For example, if, in the above example, the taxpayer had investment income and trading income in 2008/09 and investment income in 2009/10, he may offset the loss against the total income of either tax year.

Where a loss relief claim is made, the amount of the loss relieved will always be the lower of the total amount of the loss and the profits against which it is offset.

A trading loss may therefore be carried back one year, but, as a temporary measure due to the economic downturn, up to £50,000 of trading losses in each of 2008/09 and 2009/10 may be carried back three years, offsetting against the latest year first, i.e. a loss in 2009/10 may be offset against total income of 2008/09, followed by the total income of 2007/08 and 2006/07.

Chapter 4. Principles of Employment Income

4.1. Distinction between Employment and Self-employment

Many employees are keen to become self-employed for tax purposes, since there are a number of tax advantages, such as a greater ability to deduct expenses, but being accepted as self-employed by HM Revenue & Customs involves more than simply putting the appropriate documentation and business structure in place. The status depends on the nature of the relationship between the person doing the work and the person for whom the work is performed.

A number of tests have been developed over the years by the courts to determine a taxpayer's status, but these are not applied mechanically and each case is considered on its individual facts.

Broadly speaking, self-employment has been defined as a 'contract for services', whereas employment has been defined as a 'contract of service', with connotations of the master/servant relationship. A number of tests are applied to the contract between the worker and the person for whom the work is performed, which may be written, oral or implied. These are:

- *mutuality of obligations.* An employer is obliged to offer work to an employee, and an employee is obliged to carry out that work, but no such obligations exist between businesses and the self-employed;
- *control.* An employer is able not only to specify what work is carried out, but also the exact way in which it is to be carried out. A self-employed person will be contracted to perform specific tasks, but will use his professional skill and expertise to determine exactly what work needs to be carried out and how it should be performed.
- *right to use a substitute or obtain assistance or sub-contract;*
- *provision of equipment.* An employee will normally expect his employer to supply the essential equipment to perform the task, whereas a self-employed contractor is normally expected to provide his own equipment;
- *financial risk.* An individual who is in business on his own account will be taking a far greater degree of financial risk than an employee, and there is a far greater opportunity to profit from good work and sound business management;
- *part and parcel of organisation.* An employee will normally be more closely integrated into a business than a self-employed contractor. whether the worker is entitled to employee benefits and right of dismissal;
- *method of payment.* Employees will normally receive a regular salary, whereas self-employed contractors will generally charge an agreed amount for an assignment;

- *intention of the parties.* While the purpose of the above tests is to ensure that the legal form of the contract and the intention of the parties is not decisive in determining the status of a worker, it will be relevant where the above factors are evenly balanced.

4.2. Provision of Services Through an Intermediary

In the past it has been common for a worker to avoid being treated as an employee by providing services through an intermediary, typically through personal service companies (PSCs) i.e. companies which merely exist as a vehicle for the worker to provide his services, and in which he is the main shareholder and director. An associated person such as a spouse may also be a shareholder in order to comply with company law requirements. The company is liable to corporation tax on its profits, almost certainly at a rate not exceeding 21%, and the worker is remunerated by the company. The salary is a deductible expense for the company, but the salary payments are structured in a tax efficient manner in order to minimise the worker's tax liability. There is also the possibility of remuneration by payment of dividends. PSCs are still legal and they can still enable workers to reduce personal financial risk through limited liability.

Legislation now contained in ITEPA 2003 ss.49-61 was introduced in FA 2000 (preceded by the notorious Budget Press Release IR35 by which name the legislation is commonly referred to) and has removed the tax advantages of such an arrangement in many circumstances. The effect of the legislation is to look through the company, and whether an individual is to be treated as an employee or to be self-employed is determined by the normal tests relating to employment and self-employment. Broadly speaking, the legislation operates by comparing the profits earned from engagements where the worker is deemed to be an employee with the salary paid by the company. Where the profits exceed the salary paid the difference is treated as a deemed payment of salary at the end of the tax year.

4.3. Managed Service Companies

HM Revenue & Customs have found the PSC legislation difficult to administer, since it requires them to rule whether each contract falls within its scope. The Finance Act 2007 introduced legislation aimed at counteracting the use of managed service companies (MSC), namely composite companies which provide services to coordinate and administer the activities of workers who would otherwise have formed their own PSCs. These individuals will be employees and shareholders of the MSC and may be remunerated through a tax-efficient mixture of salary and dividends. The legislation looks at the activities of the MSC and is therefore simpler to administer.

Where an MSC provides the services of an individual and that individual receives a payment or benefit which can reasonably be taken as being in respect of these services and the payment or benefit is not treated as earnings from an employment with the MSC, the MSC is treated as making a deemed employment payment to the individual at the same time as the payment or benefit is made.

4.4.   Scope of Employment Income

Employment income includes any income arising by reason of an employee's employment and need not be received from the employer. A leading case in this area is *Shilton v Wilmshurst (1990) (BTC 66)*, which involved Peter Shilton, the former England goalkeeper. He was paid a sum of money by Southampton Football Club to induce him to move from his then employer, Nottingham Forest. This payment was held to be taxable since Southampton only paid the money because Shilton was Nottingham Forest's goalkeeper and it thus arose from his employment, even though it was not paid by his current employer. Payments of this nature have often been referred to as 'golden hellos'. Tips and gratuities received, for example by restaurant staff, are taxable under the same principle.

4.5.   Time of Receipt

Earnings are taxed in full in the year in which they are received. There are, however, anti-avoidance rules to prevent manipulation of this rule for tax purposes. The basic rule is that the date of receipt for tax purposes is the earlier of the date of actual receipt and the date on which the earnings are available to the employee. If an employee can choose to receive a bonus on any date from 15 March 2010 onwards it will be taxed in 2009/10, even if the employee chooses not to collect it until the end of April. There are more stringent rules for directors, since they have more opportunity to manipulate the timing of receipts.

Benefits in kind are taxed when they are received.

4.6.   Deduction of Expenses

In order for expenses to be deductible against employment income for income tax they must be wholly, exclusively and necessarily incurred in the performance of the employee's duties. The definition of whether an expense is necessary is not determined by whether the employer considers it to be so, but whether the duties could be performed without incurring the expense. This is a notoriously restrictive provision which has, however, been upheld on a number of occasions and contrasts with the rule for deducting expenses from trading income, where expenses merely need to be wholly and exclusively incurred in the course of the business.

The words 'wholly and exclusively' preclude a deduction where expenditure has a dual purpose unless the expenditure can be apportioned between a part of the expenditure which satisfies the definition and part which does not, in which the part satisfying the definition is deductible.

Examples of expenses which have been held not to be deductible are:
1. expense of a bank manager joining a club, which was a requirement of the employment, since on an objective basis the job could have been performed without incurring the expense;
2. costs of clothing, since it is possible to perform duties as an accountant, for example, without wearing a suit. The cost of uniform and protective clothing is deductible;
3. the cost of an employee of HM Revenue & Customs using his own car to travel from home to various tax offices and premises of employers in excess of the amount reimbursed by HMRC was held not to be deductible. The taxpayer was not required to use his own car and could have travelled by public transport;
4. cost of commuting to permanent place of employment, since the employee is simply putting himself in a position to perform his duties.

Examples of expenses which are deductible include:
1. subscriptions payable to professional bodies, provided these are relevant to the employment;
2. contributions, within limits, to registered pension schemes;
3. travel expenses to temporary places of employment, temporary defined as being 24 months or less.

4.7.   Benefits in Kind

Where employees are paid in kind, i.e. through means such as a company car rather than cash, these benefits are valued for tax purposes and treated as additional salary. The benefit assessable on employees is the 'cash equivalent' of the benefit, which is defined as the cost to the employer of providing the benefit less any amounts contributed by the employee. This general rule is, however, overridden by statute in the case of certain high value benefits such as cars and accommodation. The cost to the employer is defined as the additional or marginal cost to the employer. This was established in the landmark case of *Pepper v Hart (1995) (BTC 591)*, which concerned the provision of education at reduced fees to the children of teachers at a public school. It was held that provided the fees charged covered the additional costs of books and catering etc, no benefit arose. The same principle applies to free rail or bus travel for employees.

Employees earning less than £8,500 a year (known as lower-paid employees), are assessable on the majority of benefits on a different basis. With the exception of accommodation which is not job-related, the waiver of loans and the provision of cash vouchers, non-cash vouchers and credit tokens, lower paid employees are assessed on the second-hand value of benefits provided. If a benefit cannot be converted into cash no benefit arises.

The bases of valuation of some of the most common benefits in kinds are as follows:

Gift of asset	Cost of asset to employer, less amount paid by employee.
Loan of asset	Annual charge of 20% of cost of asset to employer, less amount paid by employee.
Accommodation	No charge if accommodation is job-related.
	Otherwise charge of annual value (a notional based on the old rateable value), plus an additional of (Cost of property - £75,000) x official rate of interest.
	Amount paid by employee deducted from charge.
Ancillary accommodation costs, e.g. utility costs	Cost to employer.
	Furniture provided charged at 20% of cost p.a.
	Charge capped at 10% of salary, if accommodation is job-related.
	Amount paid by employee deducted from charge.
Car	Percentage of cost.
	Percentage varies between 15% and 35%, depending on emissions' rating of car.

	Amount paid by employee deducted from charge.
Fuel	Percentage used for car benefit x notional figure (£19,400 for 2009/10).
	To avoid charge, employee must be require to, and must actually, make full reimbursement.
	No reduction in charge if partial reimbursement is made.
Loan	Amount outstanding x official rate of interest.
	Interest paid by employee deducted from charge.

Chapter 5. Property Income

5.1. Introduction

Property income covers all income from furnished and unfurnished property situated in the UK. It is not treated as trading income, even if it is being run in an organised fashion as a trade (income from property situated overseas is taxed using the same rules, but is treated as foreign income).

Property income includes casual receipts from letting, even if a business is not being run on an organised basis. Chargeable gains incurred in the course of letting are not treated as property income.

Tax is charged on the total profit arising on the letting of qualifying properties during the tax year itself. The income from all properties let by a taxpayer is pooled. Therefore, a loss arising on one property may be offset against the profit arising on other properties. The monthly or quarterly rental income is taxed on an accruals basis.

5.1.1. Lease Premiums

Where a lease of 50 years or less is granted during the year, a portion of any premium received by the landlord or any person connected with him is taxable as property income. The portion is given by the formula:

$$\text{Premium} \quad x \quad \frac{50 - n}{50}$$

Where n is the number of years for which the lease has been granted (other than the first).

Where the lease is granted to a trader, the lessee can obtain a deduction from his trading income for the portion of the lease premium which is taxable in the hands of the lessor, but this deduction must be spread over the term of the lease. In the above example, Owen can, therefore, obtain a deduction of £168 for each of the 30 years. In the year the lease is granted the relief is given pro-rata, calculated to the nearest month, i.e. in the year ended 31 December 2009 Owen will claim £168 x 4/12 = £56.

5.2. Expenditure Deductible

Expenditure incurred wholly and exclusively in the course of letting may be deducted from the rent receivable, if it is a proper debit item under normal accounting principles and is not prohibited by statute. Examples include:
- repairs and maintenance;
- wages of porters and maintenance staff;

- cost of collecting rent;
- legal and accountancy fees;
- insurance;
- ground rent;
- service charges not recoverable from tenant;
- interest on loan to purchase property.

5.3.   Relief for Capital Expenditure

Capital allowances are available on plant and machinery used in the running of a letting business, and the computation uses an accounting date of 5 April. Capital allowances are not normally available on plant and machinery used in a dwelling. Therefore, they are not available on the cost of furniture in a furnished property. Relief for furniture is claimed on one of the following bases:

Renewals basis

No relief is available on the cost of furniture first used in the property, but the cost of replacement furniture is deductible as a revenue expense in the period in which it is incurred. The cost of furniture attributable to an improvement is, however, not deductible.

Wear and tear basis

Using this basis, the actual cost of the furniture is ignored and in each period an allowance may be claimed of 10% of the rent receivable during the period less payments to the landlord for services which would normally be borne by the tenant, e.g. Council Tax and water rates. In addition an allowance may be given for the renewal of fixtures which are an integral part of the building, e.g. washbasins, toilets.

Whichever basis is chosen it must be applied consistently. Most landlords will probably choose the wear and tear basis, because they incur considerable expenditure on furniture when the property is let for the first time. This expenditure is not deductible under the renewals basis, and it will probably be a number of years before any of the items have to be replaced.

5.4.   Losses

The profits and losses from each property are pooled, so that the property income assessment will be the net profit from all the properties. If there is a net loss, this will be carried forward and offset against the property income of future years.

5.5. Furnished Holiday Lettings

Income from furnished holiday lettings is treated as property income, but is classified as earned income rather than unearned income. This has a number of advantages:

- the same loss reliefs are available as for trading losses (see section 3.7).
- capital allowances are available on furniture, rather than the renewals or wear and tear basis;
- Capital Gains Tax reliefs which are available to traders may be claimed.

All the furnished holiday lettings of the taxpayer are treated as a single business and must be calculated separately from the liability from other property income.

To qualify as furnished holiday lettings these conditions must be fulfilled:

- the properties must be let on a commercial basis with a view to realising profits;
- the property must be available for letting for at least 140 days during the year;
- the property must be actually let for at least 70 days;
- a property must not be in 'long-term occupation', i.e. let to the same occupant for a continuous period of more than 31 days, for more than 155 days in a year. This does not include situations where a property is in the same occupation for more than 31 days continuously for reasons which are not normal e.g. illness.

Chapter 6. Corporation Tax

6.1. Scope of Corporation Tax

Corporation tax was introduced in 1965; before that date companies paid income tax on their profits. Unlike income tax, corporation tax is payable on all profits, including gains of a capital nature. Indeed, a number of changes to corporation tax over the last 15 years or so, such as the loan relationships provisions, which concern the taxation of interest, have blurred the distinction between capital and revenue which is so important to income tax.

6.2. Basis of Assessment

Companies are taxed on the profits of a chargeable accounting period (CAP). Where a company prepares accounts for a period of 12 months the CAP will be the same as the accounting period. If a company changes its accounting date and prepares accounts for a period of less than 12 months, the CAP will also be the same as an accounting period. A CAP may not exceed 12 months. Therefore, if a company prepares accounts for a period of more than 12 months the accounting period is split into two CAPS, the first covering the first 12 months and the second the balance of the accounting period. The rate of tax payable is determined for a financial year (FY), which runs from 1 April to the following 31 March. A financial year is referred to by the calendar year in which it commences. Therefore, the financial year running from 1 April 2009 to 31 March 2010 is known as FY 2009. This is no equivalent of the basis year rules used in income tax, and so, where a company has an accounting date other than 31 March, an accounting period will straddle two financial years. In this case the profits are time-apportioned between the two financial years and each portion of the profits is taxed according to the rates of that year, i.e. if a company has a year end of 30 September, 6/12 of the profits of the year ended 30 September 2009 will be taxed at the rate applicable for FY 2008 and 6/12 at the rate applicable to FY 2009.

6.3. Computation of Liability

A company's taxable profits are calculated by aggregating their taxable profits from all sources, including gains of a capital nature (known as chargeable gains). Dividends received from other UK companies are not taxable because they are paid out of taxed profits, but they are relevant in determining the rate of tax paid on other profits.

Unlike individuals, companies are taxed at a single rate on their entire taxable profits; there is no equivalent of the personal allowance and no bands equivalent to the starting rate, basic rate and higher rate. The rate applicable is determined by the level of a company's "profits". For this purpose the term has a precise meaning and is defined as a company's taxable profits plus dividends received from UK companies (other than companies within the same group) grossed up by 100/90 to include the tax credit. The rates in FY 2009 are:

Profits	Rate
£0 - £300,000 (small companies' rate)	21%
£300,001 - £1,500,000	Marginal relief
Over £1,500,000 (full rate)	28%

The thresholds apply to CAPs of 12 months. Where a CAP is of less than 12 months the thresholds are reduced pro rata. The thresholds are also reduced pro rata to take account of the number of companies in a group in order to prevent any benefit to be obtained from dividing a large company into a number of smaller companies.

The marginal rate band is necessary in order to provide a smooth transition from the 21% rate to the 28% rate. A company with taxable profits of £300,000 and no dividends will pay tax of £63,000 (£300,000 x 21%) whereas a company with taxable profits of £1,500,000 and no dividends will pay tax of £420,000 (£1,500,000 x 28%). Therefore, an increase in taxable profits of £1,200,000 gives rise to an increase in the tax liability of £357,000. This gives an effective marginal rate on taxable profits in the marginal relief band between the small companies' and full rates of 29.75%. The marginal relief is given by the formula:

Fraction x (Upper limit – Profits) x $\frac{\text{Taxable profits}}{\text{Profits}}$

The fraction is set each year in the budget and is currently 7/400.

Example
Brown Ltd has no associated companies and has taxable profits of £1,000,000 for the year ended 31 March 2010. It has also received dividends from other UK companies amounting to £45,000 (net). Brown Ltd's "profits" are £1,050,000 (£1,000,000 plus £45,000 x 100/90), which fall in the marginal rate band. The tax payable is therefore:

Tax	280,000
£1,000,000 x 28%	
Marginal relief	
7/400 x (£1,500,000 - £1,050,000) x £1,000,000/£1,050,000	(7,500)
	£272,500

6.4. Computation of Trading Income

6.4.1. General

When corporation tax was introduced in 1965 it largely took over the existing income rules with regard to computation of trading income. However, the corporation tax rules have diverged from the income tax rules over the years. The principal differences are:

1. there is no disallowance for the private use of assets and there is no restriction to capital allowances on such assets. The private use element is taxed through a benefit in kind charge on the employee;
2. interest receivable and payable is taxed through the loan relationship rules, for which there is no equivalent in income tax;
3. gains and losses relating to intangible fixed assets acquired or created on or after 1 April 2002, such as patents and goodwill, are taxed under the intangible fixed assets regime (IFA), for which there is no equivalent in income tax.

6.4.2. Loan relationships

A loan relationship exists when a company is a debtor or creditor in respect of a debt which either:

- arose through the lending of money in any currency, whether or not the debt is secured; or
- is a debt on a security.

Trade debtors and trade creditors do not, therefore, fall within the loan relationship rules since a trade debt arises from the sale of goods. However, the rules cover interest paid or received, whether net or gross, such as bank overdraft interest, bank deposit interest, building society interest and debenture interest.

All receipts and payments under a loan relationship are covered by the rules, including exchange gains and losses arising on a loan relationship. Payments falling within the loan relationship rules include charges and expenses incurred directly in:

- bringing the loan relationship into existence, e.g. arrangement fees;
- giving effect to transactions under the loan relationship;
- making payments under the loan relationship;
- taking steps to ensure receipts under the relationship.

The rules also cover such payments relating to abortive loan relationships and loan relationships which the company might still enter into.

The basis on which the loan relationships are taxed depends on whether they arose for a trading or a non-trading purpose. Receipts and payments relating to trading loan relationships such as bank overdraft interest or debenture interest payable are included in trading profits on an accruals basis. A company is unlikely to receive any income under a trading loan relationship unless it is a bank or other financial institution.

All profits, gains and losses arising under non-trading loan relationships are aggregated and if there is a net profit, this is taxed as a non-trading profit. Where there is a net loss, relief is available in a similar manner to trading losses.

6.4.3. Intangible fixed Assets

Gains and losses arising in relation to an intangible fixed asset held for the purpose of the trade or a property business are treated as trading receipts or expenses in the calculation of taxable profit. Gains and losses arising on intangible fixed assets not held for the purposes of the trade are aggregated and an aggregate gain is taxed separately from trading profits. An aggregate loss may be relieved in a similar manner to trading losses.

The following expenditure and losses are deductible:
- expenditure on intangible fixed assets charged to profit and loss account as incurred;
- abortive expenditure on intangible fixed assets;
- amortisation or impairment write-down of intangible fixed assets charged in the accounts.

6.4.4. Chargeable gains

An indexation allowance is available on the cost of the asset to eliminate the inflationary element of any gain arising since 1 April 1982. The indexation allowance is calculated by multiplying the allowable cost by the following fraction:

$$\frac{A - B}{B}$$

Where:

A is the RPI at date of disposal, and
B is the RPI at date of acquisition

The legislation stipulates that the allowance must be rounded to three decimal places.

6.4.5. Dividends Received
Dividends received from other UK companies are not charged to corporation tax provided that they are taken into account in determining the rate of tax charged on other income.

6.4.6. Payments to Charities
Payments by a company to charities made under the gift aid scheme are deductible from total income and are made gross.

6.5. Losses and Corporation Tax

6.5.1. Introduction
Companies may obtain relief for trading losses in one or more of the following ways:
- carry forward for offset against trading profits of future CAPs;
- offset against the total profits of the same CAP;
- offset against the total profits of earlier CAPs;
- surrender to another group company (see section of groups of companies).

6.5.2. Offset Against Future Trading Profits
This relief is identical to the equivalent relief for trading losses under income tax. The loss must be offset against the first available trading profits from the same trade and the full amount of the loss must be offset up to a maximum of the trading profits. The time limit for making a claim is six years from the end of the loss-making period.

6.5.3. Offset Against Total Profits of ohe Period
The trading loss is offset against the total profits of the period before charges. Unrelieved gift aid donations are lost. The time limit for claiming this loss relief is two years from the end of the loss-making period.

6.5.4. Offset Against Total Profits of Earlier Periods
A trading loss may be carried back and offset against the total profits of CAPs falling wholly or partly in the previous 12 months. Losses incurred in CAPs ending after 23 November 2008 up to a maximum of £50,000 may be carried back against profits of CAPs falling wholly or partly in the previous 36 months, offsetting against the latest period first.

Any loss which cannot be offset against the profits of the current period or carried back must be carried forward.

6.5.5. Property Losses

A property loss may first be offset against other income of the same CAP and then carried forward to be offset against income from all sources in future CAPs.

6.5.6. Capital Losses

Capital losses may only be carried forward and offset against chargeable gains of future periods.

6.6. Groups and Consortia

6.6.1. Introduction

There are three situations to which provisions for groups and consortia apply. These are:

- associated companies;
- group relief, surrender of losses between group companies;
- chargeable gains and transfer of assets between group companies.

The definition of a group is different in each case and there are three different types of group:

- 51% group;
- 75% group;
- chargeable gains group.

6.6.2. Group Relief

Losses may be surrendered to a UK resident member of a 75% group. In order for two companies to be members of a 75% group, one company must be a 75% subsidiary of the other, or both companies must be 75% subsidiaries of a third company.

A group may contain non-UK-resident companies, i.e. where A Ltd and B Ltd are both subsidiaries of C Inc. (resident in the US). However, losses may only be surrendered between UK members of a group.

The group relief provisions enable trading losses and certain other types of losses to be surrendered. Capital losses are not available for group relief.

Only losses of the current CAP may be surrendered. The surrendering company may surrender the losses in preference to using any other means of loss relief and need only surrender a specified amount of the loss. The maximum loss which the claimant company may claim must be reduced by any possible loss relief claims in respect of losses of the same and earlier years, even if the company chooses not to make these claims.

A claimant company may make a payment to the surrendering company in respect of the loss claimed. A payment up to a maximum of the amount of the loss surrendered (not merely up to the amount of tax saved) is outside the scope of corporation tax for the receiving company and is not treated as a distribution or charge on income of the paying company.

6.6.3.   Capital Gains Groups

A capital gains group consists of:
- a principal company; and
- its 75% subsidiaries; and
- where any 75% subsidiary itself has a 75% subsidiary, the second tier subsidiary and so on, provided that the principal company has at least an effective 51% holding in the subsidiary.

A principal company cannot be itself a 75% subsidiary of another company.

Example
1. If A owns 80% of B and B owns 70% of C, A and B will form a capital gains group. However, C will not be part of the group since B owns less than 75% of C.
2. If A owns 80% of B, B owns 75% of C, C owns 75% of D and D owns 75% of E, A, B and C will form a capital gains group since A has an effective interest of 60% in C. D and E will not form part of this group, since A only has an effective interest of 45% in D and 31.75% in E. B, C, D and E cannot form a second capital gains group with B as the principal company, since B is a 75% subsidiary of A. However, D and E can form a separate group, since D cannot be part of the same group as C.

Assets may be transferred between companies within a capital gains group on a no gain/no loss basis, i.e. no chargeable gain or allowable loss will arise in the transferor company and the transferee company will acquire the asset at the base cost to the transferor. Where a company wishes to dispose of an asset which is pregnant with gain, shortly before sale it may transfer the asset to a company with available capital losses which can be used to shelter all or part of the gain. Alternatively, it can ensure that the gain arises in the group company with the lowest marginal rate of corporation tax.

It is also possible to make an irrevocable election to deem that an asset has been transferred to another member of the group without actually making the transfer.

6.6.4.   Consortia

A consortium-owned company is a company which is not a 75% subsidiary of any company where at least 75% of its share capital is owned by companies, all of which hold at least 5% and all of which are entitled to at least 5% of income on a distribution and 5% of any assets on a winding up.

A consortium member may claim a portion of the loss of the consortium-owned company (which may be a trading company or a holding company) equal to its holding in the company or may surrender a loss to the consortium-owned company, a trading company for offset against a portion of the consortium-owned company's profits equal to its holding in the company.

6.7.   Close Companies

6.7.1.   Definition
A close company is a 'close company' if it is controlled by:
- five or fewer participators together with their associates; or
- any number of participators, together with their associates, who are also directors.

The definitions of these terms are widely drawn.

Control is defined as:
- possessing or being entitled to acquire over 50% of the company's share capital or voting rights; or
- being entitled to receive over 50% of a company's profits by way of distribution; or
- being entitled to receive over 50% of a company's assets on a winding up.

A participator includes a number of persons other than shareholders, such as persons who are entitled to acquire share capital or voting rights and loan creditors in respect of money borrowed (except a bank lending in the ordinary course of business).

A participator's holding will be aggregated with those of their associates, who are broadly speaking the close relatives and business partners of the participator and his spouse or civil partner.

The holdings of the participators and associates will be aggregated in such a manner as to produce the lowest number of participators.

Two companies are associated if:
- one company controls the other;
- they are both controlled by the same person or company.

6.7.2.   Exemptions from Close Company Status
There are a number of exemptions which mean that a company will not be a close company even if the above conditions are satisfied. These include where the the company is not resident in the UK or the company is controlled by one or more non-close companies. This means that subsidiary companies are not close companies unless the holding company is itself close.

6.7.3. Consequences of Being a Close Company

Where a loan is made by the company to one of its participators, or an associate, the company must pay a tax charge to HM Revenue & Customs equal to 25% of the amount advanced.

Where a benefit in kind (e.g. cars or accommodation) is provided to a participator and the benefit is not taxable as employment income (generally because the participator is not an employee or director of the company), an amount equal to the benefit charge which would have arisen to a director or employee earning £8,500 or more is treated as a dividend. The cost of providing the benefit is disallowable in the company's tax computation.

Chapter 7. Capital Gains Tax

7.1.   Scope of Capital Gains Tax (CGT)

CGT is payable on chargeable gains realised by a chargeable person. Chargeable persons include individuals, partnerships and trusts. Companies do not pay CGT, but instead pay corporation tax on their chargeable gains. Many of the rules relating to CGT apply to companies. However, aspects of the taxation of chargeable gains which relate solely to companies are covered in section 6.4.4.

Chargeable gains may arise on the following types of disposal:
- sale of the whole, or part, of an asset;
- gift of the whole, or part, of an asset;
- loss, or destruction, of an asset;
- receipt of a capital sum derived from an asset, even if the person paying the sum receives no assets in return, e.g. compensation or damages for injury or insurance proceeds; and
- appropriation of an asset as trading stock.

7.2.   Exemptions

Certain organisations are exempt from CGT, the main two being charities and pension funds. Gains on certain types of assets are exempt, including:
- disposals on death. Legatees inherit the assets at the probate value on date of death;
- foreign currency for private use. Foreign currency is a chargeable asset, and gains arising from currency speculation will be chargeable;
- motor vehicles which are commonly used as private motor vehicles;
- gilt-edged securities; and
- qualifying corporate bonds.

7.3.   Residence and Domicile

A taxpayer is liable to CGT if he is either resident or ordinarily resident in the UK. If a taxpayer is neither resident nor ordinarily resident, he is not liable to CGT on gains, even if they are realised on assets situated in the UK, unless the assets are being used in a trade, profession or vocation carried on in the UK through a UK branch or agency. There are anti-avoidance rules to prevent a taxpayer avoiding CGT by realising gains whilst temporarily non-resident in the UK. Where a taxpayer is both non-resident and not ordinarily resident, for five years or less, and was resident or ordinarily resident in the UK for at least four of the seven tax years before departure, gains realised after departure, but before the following 6 April will be taxable in the tax year of departure. Other gains realised whilst non-resident are taxable in the tax year of return. Gains on assets acquired whilst non-resident are excluded from these provisions. If a taxpayer is resident, but not domiciled, in the UK and has elected to use the remittance basis of taxation, gains arising on assets situated outside the UK are only taxable if the proceeds are remitted to the UK.

The definitions of residence and domicile are covered in Chapter 16.

7.4. Annual Exemption and Losses

Individuals have an annual exemption from capital gains tax analogous to the income tax personal allowance (2009/10 £10,100). Unused income tax personal allowances may not be offset against capital gains. Each spouse or civil partner is treated as a separate person, and is entitled to his, or her, own annual exemption.

Losses incurred in a tax year must be offset against gains of the tax year, even if this results in some, or all, of the annual exemption being wasted. If losses exceed gains in a tax year, the excess losses are carried forward, and offset against the net gains of the next available year. Brought forward losses are not, however, offset if this would result in the annual exemption being wasted.

Under certain conditions a taxpayer may offset a trading loss qualifying for relief against general income against the capital gains of the year.

7.5. Capital Gains Tax Rate

In 2009/10 capital gains are taxed at a single rate of 18%, although this may be reduced to an effective rate of 10% where entrepreneurs' relief is available.

7.6. Disposal Consideration

The disposal consideration will normally be the actual sale proceeds, but the market value (agreed with HM Revenue & Customs) is used in the following circumstances where:
- the disposal is not a bargain at arm's length;
- the disposal is to a connected person (broadly speaker a close relative or the taxpayer or spouse or civil partner; there are special rules for transfers between spouses and civil partners);
- the disposal consideration cannot be valued in monetary terms, e.g. a barter transaction.

7.7. Date of Disposal

The date of the disposal is generally the date on which a contract is made, not the date of actual transfer of title, e.g. in a sale of property, the relevant date is the date of the exchange of contracts, rather than the date of completion.

7.8. Allowable Costs

The allowable cost will be the sum of: the initial cost of the asset, incidental costs of acquisition, e.g. legal fees, accountant's or surveyor's fees and costs of enhancing, or improving, the asset, e.g. building an extension to a house. These do not include any amounts which are an expense for the purpose of income tax, such as insurance premiums or payments of interest.

7.9. Indexation Allowance

An indexation allowance was available to individuals on the cost of the asset to eliminate the inflationary element of any gain arising between 1 April 1982 and 5 April 1998. This was abolished from 6 April 2008. Indexation is still available to companies.

7.10. Taper Relief

In April 1998 the indexation allowance was replaced for individuals and trustees by a system of taper relief, whereby only a fraction of the gain calculated in the above computation is charged to CGT (*TCGA 1992 s.2A*). This was abolished with effect from 6 April 2008.

7.11. Assets Owned at 31 March 1982

As stated above the indexation allowance was only available from March 1982 onwards and did not remove inflationary gains of the 1970s and early 1980s from the charge to tax, and there was still criticism of the way that CGT operated. So in 1988 CGT was further reformed to exempt any gain relating to the period before April 1982 from CGT. Two CGT calculations were performed. The allowable cost in the first of these was the actual acquisition cost plus subsequent improvements and in the second the market value of the asset at 31 March 1982. If the computations produced two gains, the lower gain was taken, if the computations produced two losses, the lower loss was taken and if one computation produced a gain and the other a loss, there was no gain or loss. With effect from 6 April 2008 the use of the March 1982 value is now compulsory and only one calculation is performed.

7.12. Married Couples

Married couples are treated as separate individuals for the purposes of CGT and each spouse is entitled to an annual exemption. Where assets are jointly held the gain will be apportioned in accordance with the beneficial interests held by the spouses. Where this is unclear, HM Revenue & Customs will generally accept that they hold equal shares.

Assets are transferred between married couples who are living together in accordance with TCGA 1992 s.288(3) on a no gain/no loss basis, i.e. the deemed proceeds for the spouse making the transfer (the 'transferor spouse') is the allowable cost of the transferor spouse.

7.13. Disposal to Connected Parties

Where an asset is disposed of to a connected party, the disposal consideration will be the market value of the asset rather than the actual sale proceeds. This will normally be its open market value.

Where an asset is sold to a connected person at a loss, the normal loss relief rules do not apply. The loss may only be offset against gains arising on future disposals to the same connected person whilst they are still connected.

7.14. Part Disposals

Where there is a disposal of a part of an asset (e.g. two acres of land out of five), the allowable cost , i.e. cost or March 1982 value must be multiplied by the fraction A/A+B where:

A is the value of part disposed of; and
B is the value of the part retained.

Example

Diane acquired four acres of land on 4 May 1999 at a cost of £50,000. She sold one acre of the land on 24 July 2009 for £60,000. The value of the remaining three acres at that date was £90,000.

	£
Proceeds	60,000
Allowable Cost £50,000 x $\frac{60,000}{60,000 + 90,000}$	(20,000)
Gain	£40,000

7.15. Shares

Since shares are 'fungible', i.e. all shares in a particular company are identical, it is impossible to match the actual shares sold against specific acquisitions.

Matching rules, therefore, deem shares to have been acquired in a particular order. Shares are matched against acquisitions in the following order:

1.   shares acquired on the same day;
2.   shares acquired in the **following** 30 days. This is to prevent taxpayers holding unrealised losses on shares from selling them to realise the loss and re-acquiring them very soon thereafter;
3.   shares acquired before the date of disposal. These shares are pooled and the acquisition cost of shares sold is, therefore, a weighted average of all acquisitions.

7.16.   Capital Gains Tax Reliefs

7.16.1. Replacement of Business Assets

Businesses often need to replace business assets or move premises due to expansion, but it would be difficult for them to do so if part of the sale proceeds from selling the old asset, which are needed to finance the replacement, were lost due to the tax charge. In order to prevent this, the gain on the old asset may be 'rolled over', i.e. deducted from the cost of the new asset. The new asset will, therefore, have a lower base cost and a higher gain will arise on its eventual disposal. The gain can be deferred indefinitely, in theory, if the proceeds are always re-invested in a new asset.

The old and new asset must both belong to one of the following categories although they need not both belong to the same category:

1.   land and buildings occupied and used wholly for the purposes of the trade. This category does not apply where the taxpayer is carrying on a trade of dealing in or developing land or, if he has an estate or interest in that land, of providing services to the occupier of the land;
2.   fixed plant and machinery;
3.   goodwill;
4.   ships, aircraft and hovercraft;
5.   satellites, space stations and spacecraft;
6.   milk, fish or potato quotas and ewe or suckler cow premium quotas.

The relief is available to taxpayers who are carrying on a trade, profession or vocation. The new asset must be purchased within a period commencing one year before and ending three years after the disposal.

7.16.2. Gift Relief

Where certain types of assets are transferred by way of a gift to a person who is resident or ordinarily resident in the UK, a joint election may be made by the donor and donee for the gain arising on the transfer to be deducted from the donee's acquisition cost. The main types of transfers covered are transfers of assets used in the donor's business, shares or securities in a trading company or a holding company of a trading group, provided that these are not listed on a recognised stock exchange and transfers which give rise to an immediate IHT charge.

7.16.3. Transfer of Assets to a Limited Company
If an individual has been trading through an unincorporated business and subsequently transfers the business to a limited company, he makes a disposal of chargeable assets. The gain arising on the transfer is deducted from the value of the shares received in the company.

7.16.4. Entrepreneurs' Relief
Entrepreneurs' relief reduces the CGT rate of 18% to 10% on a material disposal of business assets, assets in use for the purposes of the business at the time a business ceases to be carried on or a disposal of shares or securities in a company. A disposal of business assets must be of the whole or a part of the business, i.e. the business disposed of must be capable of being run as a going concern and, where the disposal is of shares, the company must be a trading company or holding company of a trading group and the taxpayer must have held at least 5% of the share capital for at least one year prior to the disposal.

7.16.5. Principal Private Residence Relief
Any capital gain arising when a taxpayer sells his principal private residence is exempt and no loss is allowable. The entire gain is exempt only if there has been actual or deemed occupation throughout the period of ownership, otherwise only a portion of the gain is exempt on a time-apportionment basis. The gain relating to the last three years of ownership is normally exempt. Deemed occupation means that the taxpayer is treated as if they were occupying the property, even if they are actually living elsewhere and broadly covers periods when the taxpayer is required to live away from home for the purposes of work or in job-related accommodation.

Chapter 8. National Insurance Contributions

8.1.   Introduction

National insurance contributions are paid on trading income of the self-employed and on employment income. The self-employed pay class 2 and class 4 contributions, whereas employees pay class 1 contributions. In the case of employment income, the employer must also pay contributions, and these are effectively a payroll tax. The employee's contributions are termed primary contributions and the employer's contributions secondary contribution. In addition, employers must also pay class 1A contributions on benefits in kind.

8.2.   National Insurance Contributions and Employees

8.2.1.   Contributions by Employees

Class 1 NIC are payable on an employee's earnings during an earnings period. This period will depend on the interval at which an employee is paid, and will generally, but not necessarily, be a week or a month (irrespective of the fact that months are of unequal length). Contributions for company directors are always calculated using an annual earnings period, regardless of when payments are made.

Unlike PAYE, contributions are not calculated on a cumulative basis. Therefore, contributions are calculated on any commission or bonus by reference to the earnings limits for the earnings period in which it is paid.

The earnings on which contributions are payable include all payments in cash, but exclude most payments in kind (although these are subject to class 1A contributions by the employer). However, no deductions are made for expenses or pension contributions.

Primary class 1 contributions are payable at a rate of 11% (non-contracted out earners) or 9.4% (contracted out earners) by earners between the ages of 16 and 65 (for men) and 60 (for women) on earnings falling between the primary threshold (£110 p.w., £476 p.m. or £5,715 p.a. in 2009/10) and the upper earnings limit (UEL) (£844 p.w., £3,656 p.m. or £43,875 p.a. in 2009/10) and at a rate of 1% on earnings above the UEL.

Where an employee has contracted out of the State Earnings Related Pension Scheme (SERPS) and has taken out a personal pension, contributions at the non-contracted out rate are payable. However, HM Revenue & Customs will pay a portion of these to the insurance company providing the appropriate personal pension.

8.2.2. Contributions by Employers

Secondary class 1 contributions are payable by the employer on earnings above the secondary threshold (this is the same as the primary threshold). This means that secondary NIC paid by, say, football clubs is a major expense.

Contributions are payable at 12.8% (2009/10) in respect of employees who are not contracted out.

Where employees are contracted out, contributions between the secondary threshold and the UEL are reduced to 9.1% (2009/10) for employees in a final salary-related scheme and to 11.4% (2009/10) for employees in a money purchase scheme.

It is not possible to recover secondary contributions from an employee (except in certain circumstances involving employment-related securities).

Class 1A contributions are payable by the secondary contributor at 12.8% (2009/10) on the cash equivalent of the benefit, i.e. the benefit charge on the employee, for the majority of benefits in kind. The amount is to be calculated to the nearest penny. In general, the cash equivalent will be the same as the benefit charge on the employee.

Class 1A contributions are paid annually, whereas class 1 contributions are paid in respect of the earnings period of the employee.

Where an employee is given a cash alternative to the benefit, class 1A NIC is payable where the employee receives and retains the benefit. The liability is based on the amount chargeable on the employee. Therefore, if the cash alternative is greater than the value of the benefit using the normal rules, the liability is based on the amount of the cash alternative. Where an employee receives the cash, class 1 NIC is payable.

8.3. Notional Payments of Class 1 Contributions

There is a notional payment where earnings exceed a lower earnings limit (£95 p.w., £412 p.m., £4,940 p.a. in 2009/10), but do not reach the primary threshold.

Although no payment is made, the notional payment preserves the earner's right to benefit entitlement, such as the basic state pension.

8.4. Annual Maximum Contributions

Where a taxpayer has more than one employment, he will pay class 1 contributions in respect of his earnings from all employments. Similarly, where a taxpayer is both employed and self-employed, he will pay class 1 contributions in respect of his earnings from employment and class 2 and, if applicable, class 4 contributions in respect of his self-employed earnings.

There is, however, a limit to the total NIC that an individual may pay in a tax year. There are, in fact, three separate limits which may apply in different situations:

1. where an individual has earnings from more than one employment, contributions are only payable on aggregate earnings up to the UEL;
2. where an individual has earnings from employment and self-employed earnings on which class 2 contributions, but not class 4 contributions are payable (i.e. the profits are below the lower limit), the total class 1 and class 2 contributions payable at the main rate may not exceed 53 weekly class 1 contributions at the main rate;
3. where an individual has earnings from employment and self-employed earnings on which both class 2 contributions and class 4 contributions are payable, the total class 1, class 2 and class 4 contributions may not exceed 53 weekly class 2 contributions plus the maximum class 4 contributions.

8.5. National Insurance Contributions and the Self-Employed

8.5.1. Class 2 Contributions

Class 2 contributions are paid at a flat-rate of £2.40 per week by earners between the ages of 16 and 65 (for men) or 60 (for women). Class 2 contributions give entitlement to benefits, except unemployment benefit and the earnings-related element of the state pension scheme. There are slightly more than 52 weeks in a year. Therefore, every few years there will be a 53-week year in order to catch up.

Class 2 contributions are not payable if an earner's self-employed earnings fall below a minimum exemption limit (£5,075 in 2009/10). This is calculated on the taxpayer's total actual earnings from all self-employed activities shown in the accounts during the tax year, i.e. the adjustment and basis period rules do not apply. In calculating whether a taxpayer falls into the low earnings exemption it will, therefore, generally be necessary to time-apportion the earnings of two periods.

Class 2 contributions are paid on the basis of estimated earnings for the year, and will be repaid if it subsequently transpires that the earnings do not exceed the exemption limit.

8.5.2. Class 4 Contributions

Class 4 contributions are earnings-related and are payable on trading profits and gains.

Contributions are payable at 8% on profits and gains between a lower limit and an upper limit (£5,715 and £43,875 respectively in 2009/10) and at a rate of 1% on profits in excess of the limit.

Chapter 9. Value Added Tax

9.1.   Scope of Value Added Tax (VAT)

VAT is chargeable on a taxable supply of goods or services made in the UK by a taxable person in the course of any business carried on by that person. A transaction which does not satisfy all these conditions is outside the scope of VAT. VAT is charged on goods and services as they pass through the supply chain to the 'final consumer', but most businesses can reclaim the VAT on the goods that they purchase for use in the business from HM Revenue & Customs. Therefore, the ultimate burden falls on the non-business consumer. The term 'supply' covers both supplies of goods and supplies of services, although, in general, the term excludes anything not done for a consideration

A taxable person is defined as any person who is, or who is required to be, registered under *VATA 1994*. This can be a sole trader, partnership or a voluntary organisation such as a charity.

9.2.   Rates of VAT

VAT may be charged on taxable supplies at either:
- the standard rate of 17.5%[2], i.e. 7/47th of the VAT-inclusive price. Any supplies which are neither exempt, nor taxed at either the reduced rate or the zero-rate are taxed at the standard rate;
- the reduced rate of 5%, i.e. 1/21st of the VAT-inclusive price. Items taxed at the reduced rate are listed in VAT 1994 Sch.7A;
- the zero-rate. Items taxed at the zero rate are to be found in VATA 1994 Sch. 8.

Items contained in VATA 1994 Sch.9 are exempt and are outside the scope of VAT.

9.3.   Accounting for VAT

9.3.1. Procedure for Making Return
A return must be made in respect of an accounting period by no later than the end of the month following the end of the return period. If the total output tax exceeds the total input tax, the balance must be paid to HM Revenue & Customs by the same date. If input tax exceeds output tax, HM Revenue & Customs will repay the difference. Normally, the only businesses who will

---

[2] This was temporarily reduced to 15% (or 3/23rd of the VAT-inclusive price) in the 2008 PBR and returns to 17.5% 1 January 2010.

regularly receive VAT repayments will be those who make wholly or mainly zero-rated supplies. Where a business makes wholly exempt supplies, which are outside the scope of VAT, it is unable to register for VAT and is, therefore, unable to reclaim the input VAT.

Supplies made must be recorded net of VAT in the profit and loss account and tax computation. Purchases must also be recorded net of VAT in the profit and loss and tax computation if the input VAT can be reclaimed. If the input tax cannot be reclaimed for any reason, the cost including VAT should be recorded.

Payment of VAT is due on, or before, the last day of the month following the end of the period to which the return relates. If input tax exceeds output tax in an accounting period, HM Revenue & Customs will refund the excess provided that it is £1 or over. A payment of VAT will not be repaid if it would 'unjustly enrich' the business, i.e. the business has not effectively borne the VAT because a higher price was charged by the business than it would have charged, if it had known that it could have reclaimed the VAT, i.e. the business was able to pass on the VAT to a customer through a higher margin.

If an incorrect return is filed, a correction must be made. The incorrect return will be returned to the trader with an 'error-return notice' and HMRC may assess an estimate of the VAT due.

9.3.2. VAT Accounting Periods

A taxable person must in general account to HM Revenue & Customs quarterly. The quarterly accounting dates will depend on the taxable person's 'return period'. These are staggered as follows to ensure a reasonably even flow of returns throughout the year:

Group 1   31 March, 30 June, 30 September, 31 December

Group 2   30 April, 31 July, 31 October, 31 January

Group 3   31 May, 31 August, 30 November, 28 February

When a business registers it may request that its return periods coincide with its accounting year. The first return period commences on the date on which the trader is, or should be, registered, and may last less than three months when a business first registers or de-registers.

A business may be permitted, or directed, to submit monthly returns. The return is due within one month of the end of the return period. Monthly accounting is beneficial if a business normally receives a repayment of VAT, but it may not be used if it has registered voluntarily.

9.4.   Records and Invoices etc

9.4.1.   Records Required to be Kept

A business is obliged to maintain the following records to support its VAT return:

- business and accounting records, e.g. ledgers, day books, stock records;
- copy tax invoices issued, i.e. sales invoices;
- copy credit and debit notes issued;
- purchase invoices received from suppliers;
- import and export documentation, showing the trader as the importer, consignee or owner of the goods and the amount of VAT payable on the goods;
- supporting documentation relating to supplies made to and received from within the EU;
- debit and credit notes and other evidence of changes to amounts charged;
- a VAT account. This must show the output and input tax for the period, the output tax due on acquisitions from other EU countries and corrections to VAT in previous periods which are corrected in the current period.

The records must be retained for six years unless HM Revenue & Customs allow a shorter period, because this causes a business undue expense, or a business has insufficient storage space.

HM Revenue & Customs have the power to require the production of such information and documents as they may specify in order to support a claim for the repayment of input tax or VAT credit.

9.4.2.   Tax Invoices

A tax invoice must be issued within 30 days after the date on which the supply is treated as having been made, unless HM Revenue & Customs allow a longer period. An extension will automatically be allowed if an extension has been allowed for tax point purposes under the 14 day rule, special accounting arrangements have been agreed, or a newly-registered business has not yet been notified of its number. In this last case the invoice must be issued within 30 days of notification.

A tax invoice is evidence that the customer has paid input tax, and an invoice must be raised if:

- a supply of zero-rated, reduced-rated or standard-rated goods is made to a taxable person in the UK;
- a supply of zero-rated, reduced-rated or standard-rated goods is made to a registered or a non-taxable person in another EU country;

- a distance sale of goods, e.g. mail order, is made to unregistered persons in another EU country.

Retailers do not need to provide a VAT invoice unless the customer requests one.

A tax invoice must contain the following information:
- invoice number;
- supplier's name, address and registration number. In the case of a supply to a person in another EU country, the number must be prefixed by the country code 'GB';
- time of supply;
- date of issue of document;
- customer's name and address;
- type of supply, e.g. sale or HP, loan, exchange, hire, lease, rental;
- description and quantity of goods or services provided;
- cost excluding VAT. If a number of goods and services are supplied these must be analysed between different categories of supplies;
- rate of any cash discount offered;
- total VAT payable;
- in the case of a supply to a person in another EU country, the alphabetical code of the country in which the customer is registered.

Where an invoice includes a mixture of standard-rated, reduced-rated, zero-rated and exempt supplies, each supply, and the attributable VAT, must be identified separately.

Where a supply made by a retailer does not exceed £100, is not made to a person in another EU country and a customer does not request a full tax invoice a modified tax invoice may be issued. This must contain:

Chapter 1: supplier's name, address and registration number;
Chapter 2: time of supply;
Chapter 3: description and quantity of goods or services provided;
Chapter 4: cost of supply, including VAT;
Chapter 5: rate of VAT charged.

The invoice must not contain any exempt supplies.

9.4.3. Credit and Debit Notes
Where there is a genuine error, or an agreed reduction in the value of the supply, a credit or debit note must be issued within one month of the error being discovered, or the reduction being agreed.

9.4.4. Purchase Invoices

In order to reclaim input tax, a business must hold a tax invoice from the supplier, with the exception of:
- telephone calls from public or private telephones;
- purchases from coin-operated machines;
- car parking charges;
- a single or return standard-rated toll charge, e.g. for the Severn bridge. A receipt is required if a book of such tickets is purchased, or payment is made in advance, or in arrears by the raising of an invoice.

9.5. Valuation of Supplies

Where consideration is given in money, the value of the supply is the amount of consideration given. If consideration is not, or not wholly, in money, it is necessary to establish the monetary value of the non-monetary consideration given and to multiply this value by the appropriate VAT fraction (7/47 for standard-rated supplies and 1/21 for reduced-rated supplies). It was held in *Naturally Yours Cosmetics Ltd v C&E Commissioners (No. 2) (1988) (STC 879)* that a supply is valued at the amount of the payment which the vendor would normally have accepted for the supply. This is necessarily a subjective figure and will not necessarily be the same as the open market valuation.

9.6. Tax Point

The tax point is the date on which a supply is deemed to arise for VAT purposes. This will affect the period in which the VAT is accounted for, and possibly the rate at which VAT is charged.

The basic tax point for goods is the earliest of the date:
- on which ownership passes to the customer;
- a tax invoice is issued to the customer;
- payment is made by the customer.

The tax point for an exempt supply is determined using the normal rules, with the exception that the references to VAT invoices do not apply, since an invoice relating to an exempt supply is not a tax invoice.

Where a tax invoice is issued within 14 days from the date of a sale, the date of the tax invoice will become the tax point, unless the business elects for the tax point to be the normal tax point. This period may be extended if the business issues invoices monthly.

The basic tax point for services is earliest of:
- the date on which the service is provided;
- the date on which the invoice is issued ; and

- the date on which payment is made.

In practice, the 14 day rule also applies to services. In the case of continuous services, e.g. utilities and maintenance contracts, the tax point is the earliest date on which the invoice is issued.

9.7. Place of Supply

A supply of services is generally made in the country in which a supplier belongs i.e. has its business establishment, or, if it has no fixed business establishment, its permanent residence. If it has business establishments in more than one country, the place of supply is the country of the business establishment which is most directly concerned with the supply. Where a supply is deemed to have been made by the recipient, the place of supply is the business establishment which most directly uses the service.

Goods are supplied in the UK if they are in the UK and the supply does not involve the removal of the goods from, or to, the UK.

9.8. Special Types of Supply

9.8.1. Mixed and Composite Supplies

A mixed supply arises where a number of different goods and services, which are taxable at different rates, are supplied at an inclusive price. The sale price must be apportioned between the various elements and tax charged on each element at the appropriate rate.

A composite supply arises where a number of different goods and services are supplied in a single supply at an inclusive rate and it is not possible to apportion the price between the different elements. It is treated as a single supply and the VAT rate charged is determined by the nature of the supply.

9.8.2. Reverse Charge Supplies

Certain services, such as legal and accountancy services and supplies of staff and supplies of electricity and gas, and some other services received from outside the UK give rise to a reverse charge, i.e. the supply is treated as if it had been made where it is received by the customer. The supply is valued at the amount of consideration given, or, if the consideration did not wholly consist of money, the amount of the money equivalent. The VAT is payable regardless of whether the business is VAT-registered in the UK.

9.8.3. Imports from EU Countries

Provided both the purchaser and vendor are VAT registered, a UK customer must pay VAT on goods imported into the UK, but may later reclaim this. If the UK customer is not VAT registered, he must notify HM Revenue &

Customs of the acquisition at the time of purchase, or the time of import, if later, giving the following details:
- name and address of person acquiring the goods;
- date of acquisition;
- date of import into the UK;
- value of goods, including any excise duty payable;
- amount of VAT payable.

HMRC will arrange for the VAT to be collected under a special procedure.

9.8.4. Exports to EU Countries
Exports from the UK are zero-rated provided:
- both the supplier and customer are VAT registered;
- the supplier's registration number includes the prefix on the tax invoice;
- the supplier has documentary evidence that the goods have been exported;
- the goods must be exported within three months of the date of supply (six months where the goods are to be used in processing or incorporation before export);
- the goods must not fall within the second hand goods scheme where the supplier has opted to tax on the profit margin.

If these conditions are not met the supply is made at the same rate as that applicable to a similar supply within the UK.

9.8.5. Imports From Outside the EU
VAT is chargeable where goods are imported from outside the EU, or removed from a bonded warehouse. This is chargeable irrespective of whether the importer is VAT registered, or whether the goods are imported via a EU country, but if the importer is VAT registered it can reclaim the VAT provided that the goods were imported in the course of business.

9.8.6. Export of Goods to Outside the EU
Goods exported outside the EU are zero-rated, provided that the vendor has documentary proof of export outside the UK, the proof of export and all records of the transaction are retained by the exporter, the goods are not sent to a UK customer at a UK address or collected by the customer even if it is claimed that the goods will subsequently be exported and the goods must not be used in the UK before they are exported.

9.8.7. Land and Buildings – Option to Tax
Supplies of land and buildings may be standard-rated, reduced-rated, zero-rated or exempt, but a business may elect to treat certain supplies of land which would normally be exempt as being standard-rated. If an election is

made, a business may therefore reclaim the input tax related to these supplies. If a business elects to tax a particular property, it must charge tax on all future supplies in relation to that property unless the election is revoked or the supply is covered by an exemption.

9.8.8. Business Gifts

A gift of business assets is a supply of goods unless it is made in the ordinary course of business, and goods costing the donor no more than a total of £30 are given to a donee during any twelve-month period *(VATA 1994 Sch. 4 para. 5(2), (2A))* or consists of samples, free food and drink to employees by way of catering or accommodation for employees in a hotel or free fuel for employees for private motoring;

The input tax incurred on the acquisition of business gifts is deductible.

The gift of services is not generally a taxable supply provided that the recipient is not required to provide anything in return.

9.9. Input Tax on Special Types of Inputs

9.9.1. Goods Not Used Wholly for Business Purposes

The VAT on goods not used wholly for business purposes must be apportioned between VAT attributable to business use and VAT attributable to non-business use. Only the former may be reclaimed as input tax.

9.9.2. Business Entertaining

Input VAT on business entertaining is not recoverable. The definition of business entertaining is the same as the definition for deducting the cost from trading income. Input VAT on staff entertaining is deductible unless it is incidental to the entertainment of others.

9.9.3. Motor Cars

The input VAT on motor cars is not reclaimable unless they are:
- purchased for resale;
- purchased for use in taxi firms, car-rental firms or driving schools;
- purchased for leasing;
- solely for business use.

In order to reclaim all the VAT it is necessary to demonstrate that the car cannot, or cannot realistically, be used for private purposes.

VAT may be recovered on repairs and maintenance costs if a vehicle is used for business purposes, even if the vehicle is also used for private motoring and even where no VAT is reclaimed on fuel. VAT cannot be reclaimed on repairs to a vehicle used solely for private motoring by a sole trader or partner.

9.9.4. Car Fuel

Where fuel is provided and there is an element of private use, input tax may be treated in one of the following ways:

- the input tax may be reclaimed in full and output tax charged on the portion relating to private use. This is calculated by multiplying a scale charge set by a Statutory Instrument the VAT fraction (7/47);

- input VAT may be reclaimed on the portion of the fuel used for business motoring. No scale charge applies if this method is used. Detailed mileage records should be retained to support such a calculation;

- no input tax is reclaimed on the purchase of the fuel and no scale charge applies.

9.10. Registration and De-registration

9.10.1. Compulsory Registration

A 'taxable person' is a person who may be obliged to register for VAT if his supplies exceed the registration threshold. The term refers to any business who makes or who intends to make taxable supplies in the course of business and which is either registered for VAT, intends to register for VAT or ought to be registered for VAT and covers individuals, partnerships and companies. Even if a taxable person is not obliged to register, he may do so voluntarily.

A taxable person is obliged to register for VAT if:

- at the end of a month his total taxable supplies over the previous 12 months have exceeded a certain threshold (£68,000 from 1 May 2009). He must register within 30 days of the end of the month in which the threshold is exceeded and the registration will take effect from the start of the following month or at an earlier date agreed with HM Revenue & Customs;

- at any time he has reason to believe that he will make taxable supplies exceeding the threshold in the following 30 days. He must register before the end of the 30-day period;

- he acquires another business as a going concern; it takes over the registration of the vendor and is therefore registered for VAT from the outset.

Example

Elizabeth commenced trading on 1 October 2008. Her taxable supplies until December 2008 were £3,000 per month, from January to April 2009 her taxable supplies were £5,000 per month and her taxable supplies were £10,000 per month thereafter.

Month	Taxable Supplies	Cumulative
October 2008	£3,000	£3,000
November 2008	£3,000	£6,000
December 2008	£3,000	£9,000
January 2009	£5,000	£14,000
February 2009	£5,000	£19,000
March 2009	£5,000	£24,000
April 2009	£5,000	£29,000
May 2009	£10,000	£39,000
June 2009	£10,000	£49,000
July 2009	£10,000	£59,000
August 2009	£10,000	£69,000

Elizabeth must register by 30 September and registration will take effect from 1 October 2005, or an earlier date if agreed.

9.10.2. Voluntary Registration

A taxable person may register voluntarily even if he is not obliged to do. Voluntary registration has the disadvantage of involving the business with all the paperwork associated with VAT, but has the following advantages:

- it may give an impression of the business being larger than is, in fact, the case;
- the business can reclaim VAT on purchases. This can benefit a business if it makes wholly or mainly zero-rated supplies or if its customers are themselves registered for VAT.

9.10.3. Failure to Register

A taxable person who is required to register, but fails to do so, is liable to a penalty. In addition he is liable to account for VAT from the date on which he was liable to be registered.

9.10.4. De-registration

A taxable person may either de-register voluntarily or be compulsorily de-registered by HM Revenue & Customs.

1. A taxable person may de-register voluntarily if he can satisfy HMRC that his taxable supplies in the following 12 months will not exceed a threshold (£66,000 from 1 May 2009);

2. A taxable person will be de-registered if HMRC are satisfied that he no longer makes, and no longer intends to make, taxable supplies or there is a

change in the legal status of the business, e.g. from a sole trader to a company.

If a taxable person who has registered voluntarily wishes to de-register, or is no longer eligible to register because he has ceased to make, and no longer intends to make, taxable supplies, he must notify HMRC in writing within 30 days, stating, if appropriate, the date on which he ceased to make taxable supplies. On de-registration he must pay VAT on any fixed assets and stock held at the date of de-registration on which VAT had previously been reclaimed unless the charge does not exceed £1,000 and or the business is sold as a going concern to another taxable person.

9.11.   Bad Debt Relief

Where a trader accounts for VAT on a sale which later turns out to be a bad debt, the VAT may be reclaimed provided that at least six months have elapsed since the later of the date of supply and the date payment was due and has been written off in the accounts.

9.12.   Special Schemes

9.12.1. Annual Accounting

A business may apply to submit a VAT return annually if it has been registered for at least 12 months at the date of application and has reason to believe that its turnover in the 12 months following the date of application will not exceed £1,350,000 (net).

HM Revenue & Customs may refuse permission for a business to use the scheme if it is necessary to protect revenue or if a business is insolvent, or its VAT debt is rising.

The first accounting period will normally run from the first day of the accounting period in the year in which the application is made to the accounting date chosen by the trader in the application. For example, if a business which currently prepares its returns for calendar quarters applies to join the scheme on 15 January 2009 and chooses 30 September as its accounting date, the first transitional period will run from 1 January 2009 to 30 September 2009.

9.12.2. Cash Accounting

A business may apply to account for VAT on a cash basis rather than an accruals basis provided that it has reasonable grounds to believe that its value of taxable supplies in the following 12 months will not exceed £1,3500,000 (net), its VAT returns are up to date, no VAT, interest, penalties or surcharges are due or, if there are such arrears, the business has agreed an arrangement for them to be paid over a specified period by instalments, it has not been convicted of a VAT offence, accepted an offer to compound proceedings in relation to a VAT offence, or been expelled from the scheme within the last three years and it has not been denied access to, or had access withdrawn by, the scheme by HM Revenue & Customs within the last three years.

HM Revenue & Customs may deny access to the scheme in order to protect the revenue.

Under the cash accounting scheme output tax must be accounted for in the period in which payment is received and input tax is accounted for on the date of payment.

9.12.3. Flat-Rate Scheme

Where a business makes annual taxable supplies of £150,000 (net) or less and total supplies, i.e. including exempt supplies, of £187,500 or less, it may elect to calculate its VAT liability as a 'flat-rate percentage' of its 'relevant turnover' for the period. The percentage to be used depends of the nature of the trader's business.

9.12.4. Second Hand Goods Scheme

Where goods are sold second hand to a taxable person it would be possible for tax to be charged twice on the same goods. In order to overcome this, an order may be made by the Treasury to reduce the VAT on a second and subsequent sale. The scheme covers the second-hand goods other than precious metals and stones.

The scheme may be used if a business has acquired the items:
- on a supply where no VAT was chargeable, e.g. from a private individual;
- on a supply on which VAT was charged under a margin scheme;
- under a transaction which was treated as neither a supply of goods nor a supply of services. Where this transaction was the acquisition of a trade as going concern, the business must have been acquired from a 'relevant predecessor', i.e. a person who acquired the goods under a margin scheme;
- in the case of works of art acquired from another EU country, from the creator or his heir;
- in the case of works of art, collectors' items or antiques, by importing them itself.

Chapter 10. Stamp Duty Land Tax

10.1.   Scope of Tax

Stamp duty land tax (SDLT) was introduced on 1 December 2003 to replace stamp duty on land transactions. SDLT is charged on transactions, rather than documents, therefore many of the avoidance schemes devised to avoid stamp duty under the old regime will be ineffective. SDLT is chargeable on 'land transactions', which are defined as the 'acquisition of a chargeable interest'. This includes any estate, interest, right or power over land in the UK or the benefit of any obligation, restriction or condition affecting the value of an estate or interest. Examples of such interests are:

- transfers of freehold and leasehold interests;
- grants of leases (including missives to let in Scotland);
- contracts for land transactions which are substantially performed before completion and the transfers of such contracts;
- grant or assignment of minor interests in land, e.g. right of way, easements, rights of light and rights of support.

10.2.   Substantial Performance

A chargeable transaction also includes the situation where there is an exchange of contracts, so that the contract is 'substantially performed'', but formal completion does not takes place. This means of avoiding stamp duty was known as 'resting on contract'. 'Substantially performed' means that either:

- the purchaser or a person connected with the purchaser takes possession of the whole or substantially the whole, of the subject matter of the contract (the 'possession test'); or
- a substantial amount of the consideration is paid or provided (the 'payment test').

'Substantially the whole' is defined by HM Revenue & Customs as being 90% or more of the whole consideration, unless the circumstances of the transaction are such that, in substance, the whole of the consideration has been paid or provided.

10.3.   Date of Transaction

A charge to SDLT is triggered, and an obligation to file a land transaction return arises, when a contract is substantially performed. If a contract is substantially performed before completion, both the substantial performance and the completion are notifiable events and SDLT may also arise on the completion, if this is greater that the SDLT arising on the substantial performance. If a transaction is substantially performed, but is subsequently cancelled or annulled, for any reason, the appropriate proportion of SDLT is refunded.

10.4. Chargeable Consideration

The chargeable consideration is the consideration (including VAT) given by the purchaser, or a person connected with the purchaser, whether directly or indirectly, in money or in money's worth. A peppercorn is not treated as chargeable consideration. The payment of the vendor's costs is treated as chargeable consideration.

Where consideration is attributable to two or more land transactions, or to both a land transaction and another transaction (e.g. the acquisition of chattels such as fixtures) apportionment of the consideration must be made.

10.5. Transfer of Land and Building at Market Value

The chargeable consideration is deemed to be at least the market value of the property transferred (or the market value rent if a lease is granted) where:
- the purchaser is a company; and
- the vendor and the purchaser are connected; and
- some, or all, of the consideration for the transfer is in shares.

The consequences of this section is that SDLT is payable on the transfer of land and buildings on incorporation.

10.6. Surrender and Re-grant of Lease

If a lease is surrendered and a new lease is granted between the same parties, the surrender of the old lease is not treated as consideration for the grant of the new lease. Therefore, SDLT is calculated on the consideration excluding the value of the old lease *(FA 2003 Sch.17A paras. 9 & 16)*. The rent payable under the new lease which is treated as consideration is reduced by the net present value (NPV) of the rent of the old lease during the 'overlap period', i.e. the period between the date the new lease is granted and the date the old lease would have expired.

10.7. Exchange of Properties

If two properties are exchanged each transfer is treated as a separate transaction. This is a change from the old stamp duty provisions, under which stamp duty was only payable by reference to the value of the more expensive property. Exchanges of minor interests are only chargeable by reference to any consideration other than the disposal, or disposals, given in exchange for the acquisitions, i.e. the element of exchange is disregarded *(FA 2003 s.47 & Sch. 4 para. 5)*.

10.8. Options

The grant of an option which may require the grantor to enter into a land transaction is itself a land transaction which is separate and distinct from any land transaction arising if the option is exercised. Both transactions may, therefore, be chargeable to SDLT *(FA 2003 s.46)*. The effective date of the grant of the option is the date that the right is acquired, rather than the date on which it is exercisable. When the option is exercised, both the grant and exercise of the option are taken into account in determining the rate of SDLT payable, but the consideration paid for the grant of the option itself is ignored. The effective date for SDLT arising on the exercise of the option is the date that the option is exercised.

10.9. Reliefs

The following transactions are exempt from SDLT. The transactions must still be notified under FA 2003 s.77 and relief is claimed in the return.

1. leaseback element in a sale and leaseback transaction, provided that certain conditions are satisfied;
2. property purchased by a charity, provided certain conditions are satisfied;
3. certain acquisitions of residential property;
4. compulsory purchase facilitating development;
5. compliance with planning obligations;
6. incorporation into LLP;
7. certain acquisitions by social landlords.

10.10. Notification of Transactions

Transactions must be notified to HM Revenue & Customs within 30 days of the effective date. Payment of the SDLT must also be made. The following transactions are notifiable:

- grant of lease for a term of seven years or more for chargeable consideration;
- a grant of a lease for a term of less than seven years where either the chargeable consideration consists of a premium or rent in respect of which SDLT is payable at a rate of 1% or more, or would be but for a relief;
- the assignment of a lease, if the grant of the lease at the time of the assignment would be notifiable or the consideration for the assignment is chargeable at a rate of 1% or more, or would be but for a relief;
- any other acquisition of a major interest in land, unless the transaction is exempt under FA 2003 Sch.3, or the transaction consists of a residential

property and the chargeable consideration for the acquisition and any linked transaction is less than £1,000;

- any other acquisition of a chargeable interest if SDLT is chargeable at a rate of 1% or more, or would be but for a relief;
- a land transaction which a person is treated as entering into by virtue of FA 2003 s. 44A(3) (contract and conveyance to a third party);
- a lease to which FA 2003 Sch. 17A para. 3 applies, i.e. a lease which continues after a fixed term.

10.11. Records and Enquiries

Records relating to the preparation and delivery of the return must be retained for six years or, if later until the date on which an enquiry is completed or an enquiry is no longer possible. Records supporting a claim not made in a return must be kept for one year from the date the claim is made. Failure to do so may make the claimant liable for a fine of up to £3,000. The records required include:

- relevant instruments relating to the transaction, including any contract or conveyance, and supporting maps or similar documents;
- records of payments, receipts and financial arrangements.

HM Revenue & Customs may enquire into a return within nine months of the date of submission and may cover the question of whether tax is chargeable and the amount chargeable. The return may be amended in the course of an enquiry in order to prevent the loss of tax. HMRC may require the production of documents in the course of the enquiry and an enquiry is closed when a closure notice is issued, stating that the enquiry is completed and its conclusions.

(FA 2003 s.78 & Sch.10 para. 3)

10.12. Payment of Tax

SDLT must be paid at the time the return is submitted. If a return is amended subsequently, any additional tax is due immediately. Tax due under a determination or assessment is payable within 30 days of the date on the determination or assessment *(FA 2003 s.86)*. The liability to pay lies with the purchaser; where there are joint purchasers they are jointly and severally liable *(FA 2003 s.85)*.

An application may be made to defer SDLT if some, or all, of the consideration is contingent or uncertain or is payable more than six months after the effective date.

10.13. Interest and Penalties

10.13.1.Interest

Interest will be charged from a date 30 days after the 'relevant date' until the date of payment. The 'relevant date' is:

- where relief is withdrawn – the date of the disqualifying event *(see FA 2003 s.87(4))*;
- if an amount becomes payable in respect of an earlier transaction on the occurrence of a later linked transaction – the effective date of the later transaction;
- in the case of a deferred payment – the date the payment becomes due;
- In any other case – the effective date of the transaction.

If consideration which is contingent or unascertainable is not deferred, interest runs from the effective date of the transaction. If a payment on account is made, the outstanding amount on which interest is calculated is reduced by that amount. Interest is also due on the late payment of penalties.

If SDLT is overpaid, it is repaid with interest.

The fraudulent evasion of SDLT is punishable on summary conviction by a penalty of up to six months' imprisonment or a fine not exceeding the statutory maximum, or both. The maximum penalty on indictment is seven years imprisonment or a fine or both.

10.13.2.Penalties

The following penalties may be payable in respect of a land transaction return:

- late delivery within three months of filing date - £100;
- late delivery after more three months after filing date - £200;
- return not delivered with 12 months of filing date – 100% of SDLT due *(FA 2003 Sch. 10 para. 3(4))*;
- failure to comply with HM Revenue & Customs notice to deliver return – up to £60 per day *(FA 2003 Sch. 10 para. 5(4))*;
- if return is understated through fraud or negligence or return is not amended without unreasonable delay – 100% of amount of tax understated *(FA 2003 Sch. 10 para. 4(2))*.
- Failure to keep records – up to £3,000. There can only be one failure in respect of each return *(FA 2003 Sch. 10 para. 11(1))*;
- failure to produce documents required for enquiry - £50 plus a penalty of £30 or £150 per day if failure continues after first penalty has been imposed *(FA 2003 Sch. 10 para. 16(1)&(2))*;

- failure to comply with notice to deliver a document, provide information, or make a document available for inspection – up to £300. If failure continues after first penalty is imposed there is a further daily penalty of up to £60 per day *(FA 2003 s.93(1))*;
- fraudulently or negligently delivering or making available an incorrect document – up to £3,000 *(FA 2003 s.93(6))*;
- assisting in preparation of incorrect return – up to £3,000 *(FA 2003 s.96)*.

If two or more penalties may be imposed, the total penalty will not exceed the amount of the greatest penalty for any one offence *(FA 2004 s.298(4))*.

Chapter 11. Inheritance Tax

11.1. Introduction

Inheritance tax (IHT) is payable on transfers of wealth on death, i.e. the estate of the deceased, and certain lifetime transfers. The lifetime transfers which are chargeable are:

- transfers made in the seven years preceding death. This is to prevent tax avoidance through 'death-bed transfers';
- transfers into certain sorts of trusts in which no individual has a right to enjoy the income or capital. This is because, unlike transfers between individuals, the assets would otherwise no longer be within the charge to IHT, since such a trust may exist in perpetuity.

The key concept which determines chargeability is that of domicile. IHT is chargeable on the worldwide assets of individuals domiciled in the UK under general law, and, in addition, individuals who have been tax-resident in the UK for at least 17 of the previous 20 years are deemed to be domiciled in the UK for the purposes of IHT. Only the UK assets of individuals domiciled outside the UK are chargeable to IHT.

Most transfers of wealth are chargeable, but there are a number of exceptions, the most important of which being transfers between spouses and civil partners who are living together. In addition, there are a number of reliefs which may reduce the value of the transfer.

11.2. Valuation of Transfer

The value of a transfer is the reduction in value of the transferor's wealth. This will usually, but not always, be the value of the asset transferred. One of the most common examples where this is not the case is the transfer of unquoted shares, where the value of each share depends on the size of the holding. For example, the value of a 2% holding is likely to be relatively low, but if the transfer reduces the transferor's holding from 51% to 49%, the loss of voting control will reduce the value of the holding significantly.

11.2.1. Exemptions

The most important exempt transfers are:

- where there is no intent to transfer value, i.e. a 'bad bargain';
- transfers made in the course of genuine commercial activities;
- dispositions for the maintenance of transferor's family;
- transfers between spouses or civil partners who are living together;
- gifts to charities;

- small gifts (below £250); and
- lifetime transfers covered by the annual exemption, currently £3,000.

11.3. Lifetime Transfers

Most lifetime transfers are exempt from IHT unless they are made in the seven years preceding death. Such transfers are known as potentially exempt transfers (PETs) and are not taxed when they are made, but are taxed retrospectively if the transferor dies within seven years of making the transfer. It is often possible to insure against the possibility of a PET becoming chargeable, the premium depending on the age and health of the transferor at the date of the transfer.

Transfers are only taxable if the total of the transfer and chargeable transfers and PETs which have become chargeable in the previous seven years exceeds a threshold or nil rate band (currently £325,000). The current transfer is treated as the top slice of this total. IHT is payable on transfers above the threshold at the rate of 20% for chargeable transfers and 40% for transfers within the seven years before death. In the case of chargeable lifetime transfers on which tax has been paid at 20%, if they are made within seven years of death, a further 20% will be payable.

11.4. Inheritance Tax Payable on Death

When an individual dies the nil rate band is first offset against the lifetime transfers which have become chargeable. Any remaining portion of the nil rate band is offset against the estate and tax is payable on the remainder at 40%. As with lifetime transfers, any transfers to the surviving spouse or civil partner are exempt and, if a spouse's or civil partner's estate does not fully utilize their nil rate band, the unused portion may be transferred to the surviving spouse or civil partner to be used when they die.

11.5. Gifts with Reservations

In order to be treated as a lifetime transfer, an asset must be transferred absolutely and the transferor must not retain any interest in the property transferred. It is therefore not possible, for example, to transfer a house to your children, but retain the right to live there rent-free.

11.6. Reliefs

There are a number of reliefs which can reduce the value of lifetime transfers and of assets in the estate. The most important of these are:

11.6.1. Business property relief

Business property relief reduces the value of property used in, or shares in, a business which has been owned for at least two years prior to the transfer. The value of the transfer is generally reduced by 100%.

11.6.2. Agricultural Property Relief

This is similar to business property relief and reduces the value of property of farmland and farm buildings and cottages by 100%, provided that the property has been owned for at least two years.

11.7. Payment of Tax

Tax payable on lifetime transfers is due on 30 April following the transfer for transfers made between 6 April and 30 September in the tax year and six months after the end of the month in which the transfer is made for transfers between 1 October and 5 April in the tax year. Tax payable on death is due six months after the end of the month of death.

Chapter 12. Tax Administration and Appeals

12.1. Introduction

From 1 April 2005, direct and indirect taxation has been administered in the UK by a single body, HM Revenue & Customs, which was formed through the merger of the Inland Revenue and Customs & Excise. Until 2003 National Insurance Contributions were administered by the Contributions Agency, which was merged with the Inland Revenue. Likewise, until recently, the assessment of tax liabilities was separated from the collection of tax. The former was the responsibility of Inspectors of Taxes and the latter the responsibility of Collectors of Taxes, but these functions have now been merged and the terms Inspector of Taxes and Collector of Taxes have been replaced with the term Officer of the Board.

Ultimate control of HM Revenue & Customs rests with the Treasury, but the day-to-day running is the responsibility of the *Executive Committee.*

There are a number of offices in HM Revenue & Customs. These include:

Enforcement Office
The Enforcement Office gathers arrears of tax which have not been collected through the normal machinery and authorises legal proceedings for recovery through the Solicitor's Office.

Pension Funds Office
The Pension Funds Office examines and approves applications for the approval of pension schemes.

Investigation Units
Investigation Office – deals mainly with the construction industry.
Special Compliance Office (SCO) – The SCO deals with serious fraud cases and cases which local Officers do not have the experience to handle. It has seven specialist investigation units based in Bristol, Birmingham, Nottingham, Manchester, Liverpool, Leeds and Edinburgh, with the senior management at an integrated office in London.

Special Investigations Section – The Special Investigations Section monitors and investigates avoidance schemes which have given rise to serious evasion of tax.

PAYE Audit Unit – monitors operation of PAYE and investigates irregularities.

12.2. Taxpayer's Charter and Taxpayer's Rights

12.2.1. Taxpayer's Charter

In July 1991, as part of the Conservative Government's policy of the Citizen's Charter, the Taxpayer's Charter was presented in parliament. Whilst nothing in the Taxpayer's Charter was innovatory, it aimed to make the general public aware of their rights, the standard of service they may expect of HM Revenue & Customs and how they may complain if they are dissatisfied by presenting this information in a succinct form and in language comprehensible to the layman. Under the Charter HM Revenue & Customs undertake to be fair, to help you, to provide an efficient service and to be accountable for what it does. It also sets out how a taxpayer may complain it he is not satisfied and the standards of behaviour which HMRC require from the taxpayer.

12.2.2. Complaints Procedure

If a taxpayer wishes to make a complaint he should write to the local tax office in the first instance. If the complainant still does not receive a satisfactory reply he has various options. Traditional methods are to refer the matter either to the Chairman of the Board of HM Revenue & Customs or to his local MP so that it can be taken up either with HMRC's political masters, the Treasury, or with the Ombudsman. If it is alleged that HM Revenue & Customs have exceeded their legal powers, legal advice may be sought with a view to seeking a judicial review of HMRC's conduct.

The Taxpayers' Charter has established a further means of pursuing a complaint. Complaints that HM Revenue & Customs have not followed their internal procedures may be referred to the Adjudicator, who is independent of HM Revenue & Customs. Complaints are investigated free of charge, but only after HM Revenue & Customs' internal procedures have failed to resolve the matter. If the complaint relates to the conduct of a criminal prosecution, the adjudicator will not investigate the complaint until after court proceedings have finished. The adjudicator will ask HM Revenue & Customs for a report and obtain any further information necessary from the complainant. Normally he will attempt to persuade the complainant and HM Revenue & Customs to reach a negotiated settlement, but if this fails he will recommend a course of action to HM Revenue & Customs. HMRC are not bound to follow this recommendation, but have promised to do so, except under 'exceptional circumstances'. The adjudicator publishes an annual report and must include in it any instances when the recommendations have not been followed. The adjudicator will not investigate complaints which have already been referred to the Parliamentary Ombudsman. However, a complainant may refer his complaint to the Parliamentary Ombudsman if he is dissatisfied with the recommendation of the adjudicator.

12.3. Obtaining Advice from HM Revenue & Customs

HM Revenue & Customs are prepared to offer guidance on their interpretation of the law, Statements of Practice and other published information where they are able to do so, and in cases where there is a public interest in an industry or financial sector and the operation of the law is uncertain. They will not advise a taxpayer on the conduct of his own affairs. Where advice is sought a taxpayer must:

- 'put all his cards face upwards on the table';
- indicate the guidance sought;
- make it plain that it is fully considered guidance which is being sought; and
- indicate the use which it is intended to make of the guidance, and in particular whether he plans to tell others of it.

12.4. Errors by HM Revenue & Customs

HM Revenue & Customs will reimburse the taxpayer's costs where these have arisen as a result of 'serious' or 'repeated' errors by HMRC. These may include professional fees, personal expenses or lost wages or fees. In certain circumstances HMRC will pay compensation if the taxpayer has incurred additional costs as a result of an error.

HM Revenue & Customs will not reimburse costs arising from an enquiry into a return, even if no errors are found, unless the taxpayer can show that the enquiry was seriously mishandled and/or unnecessarily prolonged. The taxpayer should, however, use his right of appeal to prevent such a situation arising.

12.5. Arrears of Tax Due to HMRC Delay

Arrears of tax may be waived where these are wholly or partly due to the failure of HM Revenue & Customs to make proper and timely use of information supplied to them by the taxpayer so that, in the view of HMRC, the taxpayer may reasonably believe that his affairs are in order. Tax will normally be waived where:

- the taxpayer could reasonably believe that his affairs were in order;
- the taxpayer was notified of arrears more than 12 months after the end of the tax year in which HM Revenue & Customs received the information indicating that more tax was due; or
- the taxpayer was notified of an over-repayment after the end of the tax year following the tax year in which the repayment was made.

Arrears of tax notified 12 months or less after the end of the relevant year may be waived if HM Revenue & Customs:

- failed more than once to make proper use of the facts they had been given about one source of income;
- allowed arrears to build up over two whole tax years in succession by failing to make proper and timely use of information they had been given.

12.6. Self-assessment

12.6.1. Introduction

Since the 1990s the tax system has been based on self-assessment for both individuals and companies. Under this system HM Revenue & Customs do not make any enquiries into a return when it is submitted, but may subsequently do so within a certain period. HMRC may now enquire into returns on a random basis rather than only when they have grounds to believe that there are irregularities.

12.6.2. Submission of Return

HM Revenue & Customs may require any taxpayer to complete and submit a tax return. However, in practice many taxpayers who only receive income which has been taxed at source (i.e. employment income, interest and dividends) and who are not higher rate taxpayers are not required to do so. The return consists of a section which must be completed by all taxpayers and other sections applicable to certain types of taxpayers e.g. the self-employed and persons who receive rental income. HM Revenue & Customs will only send the sections which it believes are relevant to the taxpayer's circumstances and the taxpayer should notify them if additional sections are needed. The deadline for submitting a return is 31 October following the end of the tax year for the submission of paper returns and 31 January following the tax year if the return is submitted electronically. If a notice requiring a taxpayer to file a return is issued after 31 July following the tax year, the deadline is extended to the later of three months after the issue of the notice and the normal filing date. For example, if a return is issued on 5 September, the deadline is 5 December for the submission of a paper return, but remains 31 January for electronic submission.

HM Revenue & Customs will correct any obvious errors of principle or arithmetical errors in a return, but not technical errors, within nine months of submission. The amendments will be notified to the taxpayer, who can insist that the return remains in the original version if he disagrees within 30 days of being notified. The taxpayer may make corrections to a tax return within the 12 months following submission.

Where it is not practicable to include final figures in a return, the taxpayer should include provisional figures calculated in accordance with the best information available at the time. In these cases a return will not be considered to be incomplete. However, HM Revenue & Customs will not accept pressure of work or the complexity of a taxpayer's affairs as an excuse for not providing final figures.

12.6.3. Notification of Liability by Taxpayer

Where a taxpayer first receives income from a new source, e.g. he commences trading or has a tax liability which is not covered by tax deducted at source, he must notify HM Revenue & Customs of his liability to tax within six months of the end of the tax year in which the liability first arose. Failure to do so will make the taxpayer liable for a tax-geared penalty.

12.6.4. Failure to Submit a Return

If a taxpayer fails to submit a return there is a late filing penalty (see section 12.12.1) and the Officer has the power to issue a determination of the amount of tax due from the taxpayer. The determination must be estimated in accordance with the best information available to the officer. HM Revenue & Customs can enforce payment of this estimate by the taxpayer until this assessment is replaced by the taxpayer's own self-assessment. A determination must be made within five years from the normal due date, i.e. 31 January 2015 for the 2008/09 return. A taxpayer may however file a self-assessment which will replace the determination by the later of:

- the expiry of the above five year period; and
- 12 months from the date that the determination is issued.

12.7. Payment of Tax

12.7.1. Due Dates

A taxpayer must pay his income tax liability in instalments unless the circumstances in 12.7.2. apply. These are payable on the following dates:

- First instalment of income tax: 31 January in the tax year i.e. 31 January 2010 for 2009/10;
- Second instalment of income tax: 31 July following end of tax year i.e. 31 July 2010 for 2009/10;
- balance of income tax liability and CGT liability: 31 January following end of tax year i.e. 31 January 2011 for 2009/10.

The amount of each of the two instalments is calculated as 50% of the taxpayer's income tax liability plus class 4 NIC due for the previous tax year less tax deducted at source (including amounts deducted under PAYE).

Example

Mr Jones had the following income tax and NIC liability in 2008/09.

Income tax liability	£15,000
Class 4 NIC	£1,640
Tax deducted at source	£2,500

Mr Jones' instalments payable on 31 January 2010 and 31 July 2010 are calculated as follows:

(£15,000 + £1,640 - £2,500) x 50% =   £7,070

Mr Jones' actual liability for 2009/10 is:

Income tax liability	£16,000
Class 4 NIC	£1,775
Tax deducted at source	£2,800

The balancing payment on 31 January 2011 is therefore:

Income tax liability	16,000
Class 4 NIC	1,775
	17,775
Tax deducted at source	(2,800)
	14,975
Instalments	(14,140)
Payment due	£835

Mr Jones must in addition pay the first instalment of his 2010/11 tax liability of £14,975 x 50% = £7,487

Where a return is amended as a result of a self-assessment enquiry the payments on account for the following tax year are increased to 50% of the amended profit.

Interest is payable from the due date to the date of payment on payments on account and balancing payments made late.

12.7.2. Reduction and Cancellation of Payments on Account

No payments on account are necessary if the amount of each instalment would be less than £250 or if more than 80% of the previous year's tax liability had been deducted at source.

A taxpayer may apply to have the payments on account reduced or cancelled on the grounds that the liability for the tax year will be less than the payments on account or will be covered by tax deducted at source. Where a claim is made, adjustments will be made. However, where it is found that a claim has been made fraudulently or negligently, the taxpayer will be liable to a maximum penalty of 100% of the difference between the tax paid and the tax which should have been paid.

Interest is payable if the payments on account are reduced to below 50% of the amount eventually payable on the difference between the payments on account actually made and the lower of 50% of the actual liability and the original payments on account calculated by reference to the liability of the previous tax year. Penalties may also be payable if HM Revenue & Customs allege fraudulent or negligent conduct (see section 12.12.4).

12.8. Records which Taxpayer is Required to Keep

Under the self-assessment regime a taxpayer is required to keep records to support his returns for a certain period of time.

Where a taxpayer runs a business, all records, not just those pertaining to the business, must be retained for five years from the filing date i.e. five years and 10 months from the end of the tax year to which they relate.

Other taxpayers must retain records for 12 months from the filing date.

These limits may be amended if a return is under enquiry.

The following records must be retained:
* purchase and sales invoices;
* receipts and invoices for expenses;
* bank statements;
* accounts;
* P60;
* dividend vouchers;
* evidence of taxable benefits; and
* supporting evidence relating to chargeable assets and the calculations of gains and losses on disposal.

It is sufficient to retain the information shown on the documents rather than the documents themselves, e.g. a complete and unaltered optical image retained on disc or microfiche.

12.9. Claims

The general time limit for making a claim is 31 January in the sixth tax year after the tax year to which the claim relates, i.e. 31 January 2016 for the tax year 2009/10, although an earlier time limit of 31 January in the second tax year, applies for many claims. A claim for a relief, allowance or tax repayment must be quantified when it is made. However, it is possible to make a claim based on estimated figures if they have not been finalised.

Where a taxpayer discovers an error or mistake in a return, a claim to amend the return may be made within the normal time limit. If the normal time limit has expired, an error or mistake claim is made under TMA 1970 s.33. The time limit for this claim is 31 January in the sixth tax year after the tax year to which the error relates. A claim may not be made if a return was prepared in accordance with the normal practice at the time or an error is made in making a previous claim. So it is not possible to make a claim, for example, following a decision of the Appeal Court or the House of Lords. An error or mistake claim cannot be used to re-open arguments which should have been decided on an appeal, or where the point was an issue in reaching agreement and determining an appeal.

12.10. Self-assessment – Companies

A company must file a company tax return within 12 months of the end of the accounting period to which the return relates. Most companies must pay the tax liability nine months and one day after the end of the accounting period, i.e. a company with an accounting date of 31 December must pay the tax on the following 1 October. Large companies (broadly defined as companies with profits in excess of £1.5m) must pay tax in equal instalments (normally four) which are payable on the following dates:

1. 14th day of seventh month of accounting period;
2. 14th day of tenth month of accounting period;
3. 14th day of first month following end of accounting period;
4. 14th day of fourth month following end of accounting period.

A company with an accounting date of 31 December will pay tax for the accounting period ended 31 December 2009 on 14 July 2009, 14 October 2009, 14 January 2010 and 14 April 2010. The amount of the instalments is based on the estimated tax liability for the accounting period.

12.11. Interest and Penalties

12.11.1.Interest on Late Payment of Tax
See sections 12.7.1 and 12.7.2.

12.11.2.Repayment Supplements
HM Revenue & Customs will pay interest on tax overpaid, albeit at a lower rate than the rate charged on underpaid tax. The repayment supplement will run from the date of payment, except in the case of tax deducted at source where it will run from 31 January following the tax year to which the overpaid tax relates. A repayment supplement on overpaid CGT runs from the same date.

12.11.3. Interest on Overdue Surcharges

Where a surcharge is imposed on the late payment of tax (see below), this is due within 30 days. If payment is not made by the end of this period, interest will run from this date to the date on which payment is made.

12.11.4. Surcharges

A fixed surcharge is levied on the late payment of balancing payments and tax arising due to amendments or discovery assessments. No surcharge is levied on the late payment of payments on account. The amount of the surcharge depends on the lateness of the payment.

Date of Payment	Surcharge
Within 28 days of due date	NIL
More than 28 days and up to 6 months after due date	5% of unpaid tax
More than 6 months after due date	10% of unpaid tax

Officers may, at their discretion, mitigate a surcharge.

Surcharges are subject to interest from 30 days after issue. A taxpayer may appeal against a surcharge within 30 days of the date the surcharge notice is issued and the surcharge may be set aside if a tribunal believes that the taxpayer has a reasonable excuse for the omission. Inability to pay the tax is not regarded as a reasonable excuse.

12.11.5. Tax Deposit Certificates

A taxpayer may pay tax in advance (except PAYE and VAT) by purchasing tax deposit certificates which involves making deposits at any collecting office. Initially, at least £2,000 must be purchased and any further purchases must be in blocks of £500. The sum deposited must remain at or above £2,000 at all times. Two rates of interest apply; a lower rate where the cash is subsequently withdrawn and a higher rate where it is used to meet unpaid tax liabilities. HMRC issue a prospectus setting out the terms of the certificates, which is available from any HMRC Tax Collecting Office or from the Central Accounting Office. Rates of interest remain in force for one year from the date a deposit is made, thereafter the applicable rates of interest are those in force on each anniversary of the deposit. Interest is paid for a maximum of six years and is paid gross.

Deposits may be sent to the Bank of England where the sum is at least £100,000 with an accompanying letter stating that it is to be used for tax deposit certificates and a confirmatory letter should be sent to the Central Accounting Office stating the name and address of the depositor and the date and amount of the remittance.

12.12. Penalties

12.12.1. Failure to File a Return

1. There is an automatic £100 penalty for failure to submit a return by the due date and a further penalty of £100 is payable if the return has still not been submitted by six months after the due date. The penalty cannot, however, exceed the total tax due for the year.

2. An Officer of HM Revenue & Customs may apply to the First-tier Tribunal to charge a penalty of £60 per day while the tax remains unpaid. If this penalty is charged, the second automatic penalty of £100 does not apply. This penalty will generally be imposed where a large amount of tax is at risk, or two or more returns are outstanding and determinations have been made.

3. If a return is not filed within 12 months of the due date, a penalty of 100% of the tax due may be imposed.

4. A penalty may not exceed the total tax liability shown on the return, once submitted. If penalties have already been imposed, an adjustment will be made.

In the case of companies, the penalty is increased to £500, rising to £1,000 if the return is not filed within three months of the due date, where a return is filed late for a third successive accounting period.

12.12.2. Failure to Notify Liability to Tax

Where the taxpayer has failed to notify HM Revenue & Customs of his liability to income tax or capital gains tax within six months of the end of the tax year (12 months from end of first accounting period in the case of a company), a penalty of 100% of the tax due is charged on tax unpaid at the normal due date. This is not applicable if the liability is satisfied by the deduction of PAYE or tax at source. In most cases, employees can rely on P11Ds supplied by the employer to notify HMRC of any liability (see section 13.2.3), although there may be instances where this may not be the case.

12.12.3. Failure to Keep Records

Where a taxpayer has failed to keep the necessary records required to support his return, a penalty of up to £3,000 may be charged. Only one penalty may be imposed in respect of each return or claim. This penalty will not be imposed in every case, but a failure to keep or preserve records may instead be taken into account in deciding the level of abatement of penalties in an investigation.

HMRC have given assurances that this penalty will only be sought where there has been a deliberate destruction of documents or there is a history of a failure to keep records, and in many cases a written warning will be sent.

12.12.4. Common Penalty Regime

A penalty may be imposed where a taxpayer has submitted an inaccurate return and the errors have led either to an understatement of a tax liability, an overstatement of a loss or a false or increased repayment to the taxpayer. The error may be:

- careless, where the taxpayer has not taken reasonable care in the completion of the return and does not notify HM Revenue & Customs of the error; or
- deliberate, but no attempts are made to conceal the error; or
- deliberate, and attempts are made to conceal the error, e.g. by submitting false evidence in support of it.

Where there is more than one error, a penalty may be charged for each error.

The maximum amount of the penalty is calculated as a percentage of potential lost revenue (PLR), the percentage depending on the type of error.

Type of Error	Maximum Penalty
Careless	30% of PLR
Deliberate, not concealed	70% of PLR
Deliberate and concealed	100% of PLR

The penalty may be reduced where the taxpayer informs HM Revenue & Customs of the error and the amount of the reduction depends on whether the admission was prompted or unprompted, i.e. whether the taxpayer had reason to believe that HMRC had discovered, or were about to discover the error. The minimum penalty which may be imposed in each case is:

Type of Error	Unprompted	Prompted
Careless	0% of PLR	15% of PLR
Deliberate, not concealed	20% of PLR	35% of PLR
Deliberate and concealed	30% of PLR	50% of PLR

In order to inform HMRC of the error the taxpayer must make full disclosure, stating how the error arose, give reasonable help to HMRC in quantifying the error and allow access to business records and any other relevant documents.

12.12.5. Assisting in Submission of an Incorrect Return etc

Assisting in, or inducing, the preparation or submission of an incorrect return is liable to a penalty not exceeding £3,000.

12.12.6.Failure to Submit a Special Return, Produce Documents or Information

Where there is a failure to submit a special return or to produce documents or to furnish information, the maximum penalty is £300 plus £60 per day for each day that the failure continues. Where the return, information or documents are incorrect, the maximum penalty is £3,000. There is no liability to a penalty once an omission has been remedied or if there is a reasonable excuse, provided the omission is remedied promptly once the excuse ceases to exist.

12.12.7.Time Limit for Imposing Penalties

The time limit for imposing a tax-geared penalty is six years from the date the penalty was first incurred, or three years after the amount is finally determined, if later. The time limit for assisting in an incorrect return is 20 years after 31 January following the tax year in question. Where two or more tax-geared penalties are imposed in respect of the same tax, the total amount which may be levied is restricted to the highest single penalty which could be imposed.

12.12.8.Appeals against Penalties

An appeal may be made against the imposition of a penalty either if there is reasonable excuse for not having complied with requirements, or if the error is an 'innocent' error which is not due to fraud or negligence or if the penalty should have been capped. Examples of reasonable excuses include:

- a return posted in good time was delayed in the post due to an unforeseen event which disrupted the normal workings of the Post Office;
- loss of taxpayer's records where replacement records could not be produced in time;
- death of partner or close relative or serious illness requiring hospitalization of the taxpayer, close relative or partner.

12.13. Criminal Offences

The main criminal offences relevant to tax are as follow:

A: Under the Taxes Acts

Offence	Maximum Sentence	Legislation
Fraudulent evasion of income tax.	Magistrate's court -£5,000 or six months in prison. Crown Court - Unlimited fine or seven years in prison.	FA 2000 s. 144
Obstructing etc. Revenue officers	Fine of £1,000	Inland Revenue Regulation Act 1890 s.11
Impersonating Revenue officers	Fine of £200 and/or three months imprisonment	Inland Revenue Regulation Act 1890 s.12
Disclosing certain statistics	Fine of £5,000 and/or two years imprisonment	Finance Act 1969 s. 58(6)
Falsifying, concealing, destroying etc documents required by HMRC	Fine and/or two years imprisonment (see below)	TMA 1970 s.20BB
CGT: obstructing valuing officer	Fine of £200	TMA 1970 s.111(2)
Wrongfully obtaining or disposing of or possessing a sub-contractor's certificate	Fine of £5,000	ICTA 1988 s.561(10) & (11)
Disclosing official information	Fine and/or two years imprisonment	FA 1989 s.182

B: Under general law

Offence	Maximum Sentence	Legislation
False sworn statements	Fine and/or seven years imprisonment	Perjury Act 1911, s.1(1)
False returns	Fine and/or two years imprisonment	Perjury Act 1911 s.5(b)
Impeding prosecutions	Three to ten years imprisonment	Criminal Law Act 1967 s.4(1)
Dishonestly obtaining money etc	Fine and/or ten imprisonment	Theft Act 1968 s.15
Falsifying accounts	Fine and/or seven years imprisonment	Theft Act 1968 s.17
Dishonestly avoiding debts	Fine of £2,000 and/or five years imprisonment	Theft Act 1978 s.2(1)(c)
Forgery etc	Fine and/or ten years imprisonment	Forgery & Counterfeiting Act 1981 s.1 & 3
Cheating the Revenue	Fine and/or imprisonment	Common law
Inciting, attempting, agreeing to commit or abetting foregoing offences	Fine and/or imprisonment	Common law

12.14. Appeals

12.14.1.Appeals to Tribunals

Up to March 2009 the first body to whom a taxpayer could appeal was the Commissioners of Taxes. These were divided into the General Commissioners, who were lay persons with local knowledge and possibly experience of the tax system, but with no training in tax and who were assisted by a trained Clerk, and the Special Commissioners, who were lawyers with experience in taxation matters who heard more complex, technical cases. From 1 April 2009 these were replaced by a new system of two-tier tribunals. The First-tier Tribunal will hear the majority of cases, whilst the Upper Tribunal will hear more complex cases and appeals from the First-tier Tribunal. The First-tier Tribunal will have a dedicated tax chamber.

A taxpayer may make an appeal to a tribunal on the following matters:
- amendments to self-assessment returns or partnership statements and assessments which are not self-assessments;
- surcharges on unpaid income tax and capital gains tax;
- penalty determinations;
- decisions relating to claims.

The appeal will be allocated to one of four categories:
- 'default paper', in which the case will be decided on papers submitted by the parties, unless either party requests a hearing;
- 'basic' in which the parties argue their case on the day at the hearing;
- 'standard', in which HM Revenue & Customs must provide a statement of case within 60 days and the parties have another 42 days to exchange documents. The tribunal may issue other directions as appropriate and after the statement of case the case may be re-categorised as complex;
- 'complex', which follow the same procedure as standard cases, although more directions may be issued.

An appeal must be made in writing within 30 days of the assessment or other notice and must specify the grounds of appeal, although the tribunal may allow other grounds to be put forward at the hearing if they believe the omission was not wilful or unreasonable.

At the hearing HM Revenue & Customs will normally be represented by the Officer of the Board and either party may be represented by a barrister, solicitor or accountant. It is not compulsory for the taxpayer to attend but it is usual for the taxpayer to appear in person or to be represented by his lawyer or accountant. The onus of proof is on the taxpayer, unless HMRC are alleging fraud. The function of the tribunal is to decide the facts of the case and they are bound by precedent, i.e. if the facts are the same as a previous case their decision must follow the earlier ruling. Two cases will very rarely be identical and the taxpayer or HMRC may attempt to distinguish the case from the precedents, that is to argue that there are important differences which justify deciding the case differently.

12.14.2.Right of Appeal

If either party is dissatisfied with the ruling of the tribunal it must declare its dissatisfaction immediately, and appeal within 30 days to the Upper Tribunal.

The Upper Tribunal also hears cases of judicial review, and complex cases (such as group litigations).

An appeal against a decision of the Upper Tribunal may be made directly to the Court of Appeal and the House of Lords. The powers of the tribunal are very wide-ranging and an appeal may only be made on the basis that the tribunal has misdirected itself on a question of law.

Either party may appeal against the ruling of the Upper Tribunal to the Court of Appeal, which consists of three judges and whose decision is by simple majority. If either party is still dissatisfied, the Court of Appeal may grant leave (as from October 2009) to appeal to the Supreme Court, created under the Constitutional Reform Act 2005. This replaces appeal to the House of Lords, where the Law Lords heard their last case in July 2009. These courts may only overturn a decision on a question of law.

12.14.3.European Case Law

Whilst the Supreme Court is the court of final appeal in the UK, where UK law conflicts with European law, European law takes precedence. The highest court of appeal is the European Court of Justice in Strasbourg. Sometimes a national court may refer a case to the European Court for a 'preliminary ruling' on EU law if it is unable to reach a decision on a point.

Chapter 13. Pay as You Earn (PAYE) and Collection of National Insurance Contributions

13.1. Liability to Deduct PAYE and NIC

13.1.1. General Principles

PAYE is a system for deducting tax and NIC at source from payments to employees. The aim of the system is to ensure that the correct amount of tax and NIC have been deducted on a cumulative basis. PAYE must be operated by an employer on 'PAYE income' of employees, although in certain circumstances a person other than the employer may be liable to make the deduction. These include most payments made to employees which are chargeable to income tax. The most significant exception are:

- tips paid directly to employees, but, where tips are paid through the employer, PAYE must be operated. Where tips are paid through a tronc, a separate PAYE scheme must be set up in the name of the troncmaster. Where income tax is not payable through the PAYE system, tax is recovered by restricting the employee's tax code;
- benefits in kind; the employee's PAYE code is instead restricted.

In general, where PAYE must be operated, the employer (the secondary contributor) is also liable to deduct and pay class 1 NIC contributions.

13.2. PAYE Forms and Procedures

13.2.1. PAYE Codes

In order to ensure that the correct amount of tax has been deducted on a cumulative basis, each week or month employees normally receive 1/52 or 1/12 of the total tax-free pay due to them, and also a similar proportion of the starting rate and basic rate band. Therefore for a monthly paid employee who is entitled to the standard personal allowance and where no other adjustments are to be made, the first £540 will be tax-free and the next £3,117 will be taxable at 20%.

The amount of tax-free pay to which an employee is entitled is determined by his particular circumstances and is shown in his PAYE code. This is calculated in the following manner.

Personal allowance (or age allowance if appropriate)	X
Add: Allowable expenses (e.g. professional subscriptions)	X
Less: Benefits in kind	(X)
Untaxed income from other sources	(X)
Tax underpaid from previous years	(X)
Total tax-free pay	X

An employee's tax code is normally arrived at by deleting the last digit from his total tax-free pay. Therefore, an employee who is entitled to the basic personal allowance (£6,475), and where no adjustments need be made will have the code 647. This will be generally be suffixed by one of several letters (e.g. L) which will tell the employer how the code should be adjusted to take account of changes in the Budget. The most common suffixes are:

L Taxpayer is entitled to the basic personal allowance;

P Taxpayer is entitled to the age allowance for taxpayers aged 65-74;

V Taxpayer is entitled to the age allowance for taxpayers aged 75 or over;

BR Tax is to be deducted at the basic rate with no tax-free allowances.

Example

Emma is 40 years old and is single (suffix letter L). In 2009/10 her salary is £40,000 and she pays allowable professional subscriptions of £350, incurs deductible expenses of £200 which are not reimbursed by her employer and receives benefits in kind with a taxable value of £1,500. She has also underpaid tax of £36 in 2008/09.

Her tax code for 2009/10 will be:

Personal allowance	6,475
Add: Professional subscriptions	350
Deductible expenses	200
Less: Benefits in Kind	(1,500)
Tax underpaid from 2008/09 £36 x 100/60	(60)
Total tax-free pay	£5,465

Emma's code will be 546L.

13.2.2. Forms and Records

An employer must keep a record of each employee's pay and tax and NIC deducted at each payday. The year-end returns will be made using this information and these records will be checked periodically by HM Revenue & Customs.

13.2.3. Year-end Returns

By 31 May following the end of the tax year, the employer must give each employee who was in his employment at the end of the tax year a form P60, which shows:

- total taxable earnings;
- tax and NIC deducted for the year;
- the employee's tax code and NIC number;
- the employer's name and address.

The employer must also send HM Revenue & Customs a number of forms.

By 19 May he must send:

- Form P14 (OCR), which shows the same details as a P60;
- Form P35, which shows a summary of tax and NIC deducted. In practice a 7-day extension is usually allowed;
- Form P38A giving details of payments exceeding £100 during the tax year not liable to deduction of tax to employees who were employed for more than a week during the tax year and who have not been included on forms P14 or P35.

By 6 July he must send:

- Form P11D, which shows details of payments other than in cash, payments made on behalf of employees and not reimbursed, and earnings relating to other years for employees other than lower paid employees. All benefits are included at their cash equivalent, although where payments are made to reimburse employees for deductible expenses, a dispensation may be obtained to omit small items;
- Form P11D(b), which shows details of class 1A and 1B NIC deducted. This form may also be used to make adjustments to the total benefits liable to class 1A taken from the P11D;
- Form P9D, which shows details of benefits in kind for other employees.

Nil returns are not required, but an employer must certify that all returns necessary have been submitted.

A copy of the form P11D or P9D must also be given to the employee by 6 July.

13.2.4. Joiners and Leavers

When an employee leaves he is given a form P45, which shows his total taxable pay and tax deducted up to the date of leaving and also his tax code. There are four copies of this form, one is sent to HM Revenue & Customs and the other three are given to the employee. If the employee starts another employment within the same tax year he gives two of the copies to the new employer and retains one copy. The new employer will send one of these two copies to HMRC and retains one copy. If an employee dies, a form P45 is completed and the whole form is sent to HMRC.

Where a new employee presents a P45, the new employer can operate PAYE. Otherwise the employer must complete a form P46 to request what code should be used.

13.3. Payment of PAYE and NIC

13.3.1. General Principles

PAYE and class 1 NIC must be paid to HM Revenue & Customs by the 19th of each month, i.e. 14 days after the end of the tax month. This deadline is extended to the 22nd of the month if payment is made by an approved electronic method Class 1A NIC must be paid by 19 July following the end of the tax year.

An employer is required to account for tax and NIC payments subject to PAYE in the same period as actual payments made to the employee, even if the income falls to be taxed wholly or partly in a different tax year.

Where an employer ceases business, contributions must be paid within 14 days from the end of the tax month in which the cessation takes place. Where an employer transfers a business to a successor, the seller must pay contributions relating to periods before the transfer within 14 days from the end of the tax month in which the transfer takes place.

13.3.2. Quarterly Payment

If, at the start of a tax year, the average monthly deductions under PAYE (income tax and NIC) are less than £1,500, an employer may elect to pay quarterly on the 19 January, April, July and October. If average monthly deductions subsequently exceed £1,500, the employer may continue to pay quarterly for the remainder of the tax year. A new estimate of the average monthly deductions must be made at the start of each tax.

Interest is charged on amounts paid late and any tax and NIC contributions underpaid.

13.4. Penalties and Interest

13.4.1. Late Submission of Returns

If returns are not made on time a penalty of £100 per month per 50 employees (or part thereof) is payable. This penalty cannot be mitigated and is frozen after one year. After this time a further penalty of up to 100% of the tax and NIC unpaid applies.

13.4.2. Submission of Incorrect Forms

Where an incorrect P35 has been submitted, either fraudulently or negligently, a penalty of up to 100% of the tax and NIC not reported may be charged.

13.4.3. Interest on Tax and Contributions Paid Late

Interest is payable where tax or class 1, 1A or 1B NIC have not been paid by the 'reckonable date' at a rate prescribed by *TMA 1970 s.86*. The reckonable date is:

- 19 April following the end of the tax year (22 April when payment is made by an approved electronic method) for income tax and class 1 NIC;
- 19 July following the end of the tax year (22 July when payment is made by an approved electronic method) for class 1A NIC;
- 19 October following the end of the tax year (22 October when payment is made by an approved electronic method) for class 1B NIC.

No interest is charged on late payment of quarterly or monthly payments during the year.

13.4.4. Repayment of Tax and Contributions Overpaid

Where an employer receives a repayment of tax or contributions after the end of the tax year, interest is paid at the 'prescribed rate' (from the later of the 14th day after the end of the tax year to which the payment relates and the date of payment.

Chapter 14. VAT Administration, Appeals, Interest, Penalties and Surcharges

14.1. Control Visits

HM Revenue & Customs have the power to make random control visits to check a business' VAT records. The frequency of control visits will depend on the size of the business, whether the business has a history of breaching the VAT regulations and whether there have been any significant changes in the level of activity. The business may also request a visit in order, for example, to seek advice about a method of reclaiming input tax. Officers have the power to enter premises and examine the business records. Where fraud is suspected they may obtain a search warrant.

14.2. Assessment

The business will normally self-assess its VAT liability, but HM Revenue & Customs may make an assessment if, for example, no return has been submitted or no documents have been kept.

14.3. Appeals and Tribunals

A business may appeal against an assessment that is incorrect in law and also when it can produce evidence that the amount assessed is wrong and provide evidence of the correct figure.

A business should not simply pay HM Revenue & Customs' assessments instead of its true liability. If it does so it may be liable for misdeclaration penalties.

A dispute may be settled by negotiation with the local VAT office. A trader must ask the local VAT office to reconsider its decision within 30 days of the assessment and provide it with any relevant information which was not taken into account at the time. The local VAT office may either revise or uphold the original assessment. In the former case it will issue a revised assessment.

Regardless of the outcome of negotiations with the local VAT office, the trader may appeal to an independent VAT tribunal. An appeal must be made directly to the tribunal and not via the local VAT office.

14.4. Interest, Repayment Supplements and Compensation

14.4.1. Interest on Late Payment of Tax

HM Revenue & Customs may charge interest on VAT recovered through the raising of an assessment:

- to recover VAT underpaid or over-claimed;

- relating to VAT in respect of which an assessment has already been raised;
- relating to a VAT period of more than three months;
- relating to a period, at the start of which the business was required to be, but was not, registered;
- relating to voluntary disclosures where the net amount of the error exceeds £2,000.

Interest runs from the 'reckonable date', i.e. the latest day for submission of the return and payment of the liability, to the date of payment, *(5))*.

If a business disagrees with the imposition of interest, it may ask HM Revenue & Customs to reconsider and thereafter appeal to a VAT tribunal. The tribunal may only reduce the interest charged to an appropriate amount *(VATA 1994 s.84(6))*.

14.4.2. Repayment Supplement

A trader is entitled to a repayment supplement where HM Revenue & Customs fails to make a repayment of VAT by the later of 30 days after:

- the end of the period covered by the return;
- the date the return was received by HMRC.

The 30-day period ignores any days before the end of the accounting period to which the return relates.

The repayment supplement is the greater of £50 and 5% of the repayment due.

14.4.3. Interest Due to Official Error

Interest will be paid by HMRC where, due to their error, a business has paid output tax, or any other amount of VAT, which is not due, failed to claim input tax to which it is entitled or has suffered delay in receiving a repayment. A claim must be made in writing within three years from the end of the period to which it relates. The interest will run from the end of the period to which the output or input tax relates, the date on which the tax was paid, or the date on which the business might reasonably expect to have received the repayment.

14.4.4. Compensation Due to Official Error

HM Revenue & Customs will consider paying compensation where a business has incurred expenditure due to their maladministration. A claim must be submitted for compensation, giving details of:

- expenditure incurred;
- date of work carried out;
- time spent;
- status of person involved (e.g. partner);

- hourly rates.

14.5. Penalties and Surcharges

14.5.1. Late Registration
If a business fails to register within the required time period, the penalty is the greater of:
- £50; and
- a percentage of the tax due from the date when the trader should have registered. This depends on how late the trader registers:

up to 9 months late	5%
9 to 18 months late	10%
over 18 months	15%

The penalty also applies to the failure to notify HM Revenue & Customs of the transfer of a business as a going concern. The time limit for imposing this penalty is 20 years.

14.5.2. Unauthorised issue of tax invoices
The penalty is the higher of £50 and 15% of the VAT charged on the tax invoices. The time limit for this penalty is 20 years *(VATA 1994 s.67)*.

14.5.3. Breaches of VAT Regulations
The penalty for breaching VAT requirements depends on the type and frequency of the breach. It is not possible to impose more the one type of penalty for a single breach and where HM Revenue & Customs have a choice of penalties, they must decide which penalty to impose. In order to impose penalties HMRC must have given the trader a written warning within two years.

	Fine
Failure to keep records for 6 years	£500 (fixed)
Failure to submit return by due date	Higher of: Fixed daily penalty Tax-geared penalty
Any other breach	Fixed daily penalty

The fixed daily penalty and tax-geared percentage are:

	Fixed Rate per day	Tax Geared Percentage Rate
Basic Penalty	£5	1/6% per day
If business has breached same rule once in preceding 2 years	£10	1/3% per day

If business has breached same rule more than once in preceding 2 years	£15	½% per day

There is a minimum penalty of £50 and the tax-geared penalty may only be charged for a maximum of 100 days.

14.5.4. Default Surcharge on Late Returns

There is no penalty for the first late submission of a late return. A surcharge liability notice will be issued and the business will be liable for a default surcharge if it defaults again during the liability period. This period is stipulated in the notice and runs from the period in which the notice is issued to a date 12 months after the end of the period to which the default relates. If a business defaults during this period the notice will be extended to a date 12 months after the end of the period of the latest default. There is no financial penalty if a return shows no liability or that a repayment is due, although the period of the notice is extended.

The penalty rate depends on the number of defaults in the period:

Number of Defaults	Percentage
First	2%
Second	5%
Third	10%
Fourth and subsequent	15%

14.5.5. Criminal Fraud

This will typically involve providing false information or false documents. The maximum penalty which a magistrate's court may impose is a 12 month prison sentence and a fine of up to three times the amount of tax lost. A High Court may impose a prison sentence of up to seven years and an unlimited fine.

14.5.6. Civil Fraud

This will typically involve the business behaving dishonestly, and the maximum penalty is 100% of the tax lost. This includes dishonestly claiming a VAT credit or refund.

14.5.7. Penalties for Errors on Return

The common penalty regime described in 12.12.4. applies for return periods commencing on or after 1 April 2008 or where the return is due to be submitted on or after 1 April 2009. Errors not exceeding the greater of:

- A net under-declaration of £10,000; and
- 1% of net turnover for the period (up to a maximum of error of £50,000);
- may be corrected on the next return. Errors exceeding the above limits must be corrected on a form VAT652 or by letter.

Penalties will not be imposed if the business can show that it had a reasonable excuse, such as bereavement or serious illness of the proprietor or family member.

Chapter 15. Self-assessment Enquiries, Discovery Assessments and Investigations

15.1. Introduction

Enquiries may be made into the returns of a taxpayer under either the self-assessment provisions or by raising a discovery assessment. There are important differences between the two. In particular a discovery assessment may only be raised if an Officer has evidence of omissions or irregularities in a taxpayer's return, although a discovery assessment may also be raised if new information comes to light, even though the taxpayer was not negligent or fraudulent in the submission of his original return. By contrast, a self-assessment enquiry may be made even if there is no such evidence (although in the majority of cases there will be) and HM Revenue & Customs have wider powers to obtain information where a discovery assessment is raised. There are also a number of similarities since the object of both types of enquiries is to establish the veracity or otherwise of a taxpayer's return and many procedures are common to both types of enquiries. There are similar provisions relating to enquiries into the returns of companies.

Whilst HM Revenue & Customs have extensive powers in an investigation they must respect the rights of the taxpayer, such as the taxpayer's right to privacy so that any interference must be proportionate.

15.2. Enquiries under Self-assessment

15.2.1. Powers to Make Enquiries into a Return

Before the introduction of self-assessment, HM Revenue & Customs could not investigate tax returns at random, but could only do so if they had reason to believe that there were irregularities in the return. Whilst HM Revenue & Customs will continue to make enquiries where they have reason to believe that there are irregularities, they now have the power to make random enquiries. There are three types of enquiry:

1. Full enquiry covering the return as a whole, which seeks to address all the significant risks in the return including the risk of the return being fundamentally incorrect. It will involve a comprehensive review of the underlying records, including, where appropriate, the private affairs of the taxpayer. A full enquiry will not be reclassified as an aspect enquiry.

2. Aspect enquiry covering one or more aspects of the return, but falling short of a full enquiry. An aspect enquiry will not be reclassified as a full enquiry simply because culpable errors are found which result in an additional liability, but may be reclassified if the Officer believes that something has

come to light which indicates that more than a straightforward mistake, misunderstanding or dispute over the tax position is involved.

3. Random enquiry. A very small proportion of returns are selected for full enquiry nationally, partly as a deterrent but also to obtain a better understanding into the nature and extent of detectable non-compliance amongst different segments of the population. This will help HM Revenue & Customs to refine their strategy in the selection of returns for full enquiry.

An enquiry may be initiated either on the basis of a strategy of risk assessment, or there may be a mandatory review if a return contains certain features. The letter from the Officer will be couched in neutral language, since HM Revenue & Customs do not necessarily have any evidence of irregularities. The letter will not indicate whether the enquiry is a full, aspect or random enquiry.

If an Officer discovers understatements in the return of the current period, he may decide to re-open the returns of earlier periods. To do this he must raise a discovery assessment (see section 15.3).

15.2.2. Time Limit for Initiating Enquiries

If a return has been filed by the due date, enquiries must be initiated within 12 months of the normal filing date (31 January). Where a return has been filed after the normal filing date the deadline is the quarter date (31 January, 30 April, 31 July and 31 October) following the anniversary of the filing of the return. If a 2009/10 return is filed on 12 February 2011, the deadline for raising enquiries will be 30 April 2012. The taxpayer has no right of appeal against the decision to instigate enquiries into a return, although he may appeal against other aspects of the enquiry.

15.2.3. Production of Documents

If enquiries are made into a return the Officer may issue a notice requiring the taxpayer to produce documentary evidence supporting the figures in the return within a specified period of time. This must be a minimum of 30 days from the date of receipt by the taxpayer, although in practice HM Revenue & Customs allow a minimum of 40 days and a flexible approach will be taken, for example, if the taxpayer is known to be ill or abroad or if a figure cannot be supplied within the time limit. The penalty for failure to comply is £50 plus daily penalties for continued failure.

A taxpayer is not obliged to produce documents created for the purpose of the appeal. An appeal may be made against the request to produce documents within 30 days on the grounds that:

- the documents are not necessary;

- the documents are not in his possession;
- insufficient time has been given to produce the documents.

15.2.4. Determinations and Closure of Enquiry

Once enquiries have been completed, HM Revenue & Customs must inform the taxpayer of this and of their conclusions. The notice must state any necessary amendments or that no amendments are required. A closure notice is issued which is effective on the date it is issued. The taxpayer may apply to a tribunal for a direction that a closure notice be issued within a set time. The tribunal must issue this direction unless they are satisfied that the Officer has valid reasons for continuing the enquiry and the onus of proof is on HM Revenue & Customs. An Officer may make an amendment before the completion of an enquiry (known as a 'jeopardy amendment') if he believes that there is otherwise a risk of a loss of tax, or there will be an unreasonable delay in payment.

15.2.5. Amendments to Return

The taxpayer may make any amendment required to the return within 30 days of the conclusion of the enquiry. If the taxpayer does not respond or disagrees with conclusions of the enquiry, HM Revenue & Customs may make amendments within 30 days after the expiry of the taxpayer's 30-day limit.

The taxpayer may appeal against the amendments made by HM Revenue & Customs during the enquiry or against conclusions or amendments contained in a closure notice within 30 days of the notice of amendment.

A taxpayer may appeal against the following:
- automatic penalties and surcharges;
- tax geared penalties;
- requests for documents and accounts; and
- discovery assessments.

15.3. Discovery Assessments and Investigations

15.3.1. Introduction

Once the time limit for opening an enquiry has passed, or an enquiry has been concluded, it may not normally be re-opened. An Officer may, however, raise a *discovery assessment* if tax has not been assessed or has been under-assessed or excessive relief has been given because either:
- the Officer of the Board did not have full and accurate facts either due to incomplete disclosure or negligent or fraudulent conduct by the taxpayer or his agents; or
- an Officer at the time of making an enquiry or completing enquiries could not reasonably expected to have been aware of the loss of tax.

Fraud is the making of statements which are known to be false or the making of reckless statements, whereas neglect is the failure to do what a reasonable person would have done.

A discovery assessment cannot be raised if:

- the return was made in accordance with the prevailing practice at the time the return was made; or
- an Officer has made an error in agreeing the return or has failed to consider a point, despite being in possession of all the relevant facts and information, i.e. returns, documents and claims etc. the existence of which was known to, or could be reasonably inferred from other information by an Officer.

If HM Revenue & Customs allege fraud, they may instigate criminal proceedings, but it is rare for them to do this. A notable personality who was convicted of fraud in 1987 was the jockey Lester Piggott and in the following year the Inland Revenue attempted to prove similar charges against the comedian Ken Dodd, but Dodd was cleared by the jury. This did not mean that his tax affairs were in order. He was still certainly liable for considerable amounts of arrears of tax, interest and penalties; he was simply cleared of falsifying his tax returns fraudulently.

15.3.2. Time Limit for Raising Discovery Assessment
The time limit for raising a discovery assessment is:

- 5 years from the normal filing date for a return in the case of incomplete disclosure, i.e. 31 January 2016 for 2009/10 returns;
- 20 years from the normal filing date for a return in the case of fraud or neglect, i.e. 31 January 2031 for 2009/10 returns.

15.3.3. Reasons for Initiating Tax Investigations
If HM Revenue & Customs wish to instigate an investigation (as distinct from initiating an enquiry under the self-assessment regime) a taxpayer will normally be sent a letter indicating that HMRC believe that his tax affairs are not in order and inviting him to make full disclosure immediately. In line with the current philosophy that all organisations must be cost-effective, HMRC will only do this if they believe that the additional tax that they can recover will exceed the cost of the investigation and not just because they consider it unjust that taxpayers should be able to get away with tax evasion. It would be unwise for a taxpayer to ignore such a letter since HMRC should not take such action unless they have clear prima facie evidence of irregularities. The taxpayer will doubtless incur substantial professional fees and it is unfortunate that investigations are very costly even if the taxpayer proves to

be completely innocent or, at any rate, only minor irregularities are discovered.

HM Revenue & Customs' information may come from several sources. First, they may have received information from a third party. Whilst they must guard against malicious false allegations, many a tax evader has been undone by the vengeance of an ex-spouse, disgruntled former employee or business partner with whom he has fallen out. Secondly, HMRC may allege that the declared income or business drawings are insufficient to maintain the taxpayer's lifestyle and invite him to account for how he funds his outgoings. In one well-known instance, there was a television series where wealthy people showed off their opulent lifestyle. One individual featured had become wealthy partly through not declaring a large proportion of his income and was blissfully unaware that the programme was required viewing for HMRC. The most important factor is that any explanation must be well documented. A large legacy or pools or lottery win may provide adequate explanation, provided that there is sufficient documentation. Thirdly, HMRC may scrutinise the gross profit margin of businesses and compare it with average margins for the type of business and request the taxpayer to account for any discrepancy where it considers the margin to be significantly below the average. HM Revenue & Customs may revise business accounts using the 'business economics' method, i.e. using statistical data gathered on particular trades.

15.3.4. Conduct of Investigation

Once the taxpayer has consulted a professional advisor and replied to the letter, the Officer will often wish to interview the taxpayer, who will usually be accompanied by his advisor. During the investigation the taxpayer will normally be asked to produce a statement of his private and business assets and liabilities and/or a certificate of full disclosure. The Officer cannot compel the taxpayer to complete these but it would be imprudent for him not to do so. Failure to complete a statement of assets and liabilities would result in the Officer raising an estimated assessment and invoking formal powers. Failure to complete a certificate of full disclosure will be taken as evidence that the taxpayer has not made full disclosure. A statement of assets may also be requested when a monetary settlement is being negotiated if the taxpayer claims that he cannot pay the amount demanded.

HM Revenue & Customs have formal powers to obtain documents containing information which is reasonably required to check a return, such as invoices, air tickets and work diaries. Documents which have been brought into existence for the purpose of the enquiry or which relate to an earlier return which is not under investigation may not be requested.

A notice may also be served on a third party, e.g. a bank. The notice must be issued with the consent of a tribunal who must be satisfied that the issue of the notice is justified. Subject to certain restrictions, papers may be required from a tax accountant, i.e. any person who has assisted the client in the preparation of the tax return and accounts, if he has been convicted of any tax offence in the UK or of assisting the preparation of an incorrect return. A tax accountant may be required to hand over all his papers if the Officer has reason to believe that they contain information relevant to the tax liability of any of his clients, whether or not the conviction was concerned with the affairs of the particular client or not. A barrister, advocate or solicitor is not obliged to produce documents for which legal privilege can be claimed without the consent of his client.

A tax adviser cannot be required to produce documents brought into existence for the purpose of giving tax advice (not including supporting schedules of a tax return). Copies of a communication with a client may be required directly from the client.

Whilst HM Revenue & Customs will in general try to obtain documents by issuing orders for delivery, they have the power to obtain a search warrant. In certain cases, such as where the element of surprise is necessary, HMRC may apply to a circuit judge (or a sheriff in Scotland) for a search warrant. HMRC may enter by force if necessary. A judge must be satisfied that there are reasonable grounds for believing that the documents are on the premises and an official must give evidence on oath.

There will usually be one or more meetings between the Officer and the taxpayer and his agent. The agent will normally be invited to attend and a meeting will proceed without the agent only if the agent refuses to attend or the taxpayer makes it clear that he does not wish the agent to attend.

At some stage during an investigation it is likely that an Officer will propose adjustments to accounts to reflect an alleged understatement. The adjustment may be calculated in a number of ways. They may use statistical data, such as average gross profit ratios, ask the taxpayer to account for cash withdrawals from the business or consider whether the stated profits are sufficient to meet known outgoings.

Once it has been established that profits have been understated, a taxpayer will generally be required to produce a statement of assets and liabilities. This should contain all assets and liabilities of significant value and should include UK assets:

- of the taxpayer;
- of the taxpayer's spouse or partner;

- of the taxpayer's minor or dependent children;
- held by nominees or otherwise held on the taxpayer's behalf.

It is important that this statement be complete and it should be signed and dated and refer clearly to the date on which the assets were listed. This will normally be the end of the accounting period or return which is the subject of the enquiry, although the statement may relate to the present time. The statement is used to confirm the level of omissions and the ability to fund a settlement. If a statement is found to be false, this could undermine other statements of the taxpayer and may be viewed as a serious offence.

15.4. Settlements

Although HM Revenue & Customs have wide powers in an investigation, they generally prefer a negotiated settlement in respect of tax underpaid, and interest and penalties in return for an agreement not to invoke formal proceedings.

An invitation will be made to the taxpayer to offer a sum in settlement, which must cover unpaid tax, interest and any flat-rate and tax-geared penalties. If an offer is accepted by HM Revenue & Customs, it is binding on both parties. In most investigations a settlement will be negotiated in a meeting between the taxpayer and his advisors and HM Revenue & Customs. Although an offer may be agreed orally at a meeting, the taxpayer must follow this by making the offer in writing.

15.5. Penalties

Penalties are calculated as a percentage of the tax underpaid and HM Revenue & Customs may normally impose penalties of up to 100%. They have the power to mitigate these penalties and they take the following factors into consideration in deciding the level of penalties to be imposed in each case.

15.5.1. Gravity

An abatement of up to 40% is available if the irregularities discovered are very minor. If the case has involved fraudulent conduct only a very small abatement, if any, will be offered. Regard will be had to the size of any understatement, both in absolute terms and in relation to the taxpayer's income.

15.5.2. Full disclosure

If the taxpayer has made full disclosure at an early stage, HM Revenue & Customs may abate the penalties by up to 20%. A larger abatement may be awarded if the taxpayer has made full voluntary disclosure before he had reason to believe that the Officer was contemplating an investigation. If a taxpayer only makes disclosures after the Officer has invoked formal powers, has made incomplete voluntary disclosures, an incomplete disclosure under challenge or made disclosures at a late stage when it has been clearly established that tax has been underpaid, he will be awarded, at the most, a very small abatement.

15.5.3. Co-operation

If the taxpayer has co-operated fully in the investigation, provided all information promptly and attended all interviews promptly HMRC may award an abatement of up to 40%. If the taxpayer has delayed replies as long as possible and/or has given inaccurate and misleading information, no abatement will be given.

15.6. Criminal Proceedings

HM Revenue & Customs are reluctant to commence criminal proceedings against a taxpayer due to the high costs involved and the high standard of proof required in a criminal court and prefer to reach a negotiated settlement where possible. It is the practice of HM Revenue & Customs to take criminal proceedings in cases involving fraud where they feel that it is in the public interest to do so. They will not take steps to impose civil penalties where an offence has been taken to the criminal courts, but they may do so in respect of negligence where a taxpayer has been cleared of fraud by the court or where an offence has not been brought before the courts. Circumstances in which HMRC will consider commencing criminal proceeding include where:

- there has been collusion between the taxpayer and his professional advisors or the taxpayer himself is a professional tax advisor. If fraud by a professional advisor is discovered, the advisor's clients will unfortunately come under suspicion, even if the clients themselves are wholly innocent;
- documents have been forged in order to deceive HM Revenue & Customs;
- the taxpayer has completed a certificate of full disclosure which subsequently proves to be false. This was the reason why criminal proceedings were instigated against Lester Piggott. He had reached a settlement with HM Revenue & Customs and signed a certificate of full disclosure and written a cheque for back tax, interest and penalties. HMRC then found that they had no knowledge of the account on which the cheque had been drawn;
- the taxpayer has been investigated in the recent past;
- the fraud is particularly large;
- a person is of special status, e.g. an Officer of HM Revenue & Customs;
- another offence follows on shortly after the investigation of an earlier offence.

HM Revenue & Customs are perhaps more willing to prosecute well-known personalities such as Lester Piggott and Ken Dodd, whose cases will attract publicity and may therefore act as a deterrent.

The imposition of civil penalties is no bar to a criminal prosecution also being sought.

INTRODUCTION TO THE UK TAX SYSTEM

Chapter 16. Overseas Aspects of Taxation

16.1. Residence and Domicile – Introduction

A taxpayer who is resident and domiciled in the UK in a tax year is taxable on his worldwide income, whereas an individual who is not resident in the UK in a tax year is only taxable on income arising in the UK. Residence is a temporary state in that it relates to a taxpayer's particular circumstances in a tax year. Unfortunately, deciding whether an individual is resident in the UK is not a simple matter of looking up a statutory definition, but is complicated by HM Revenue & Customs' practice. Two further concepts which are relevant to taxation are ordinary residence and domicile. Ordinary residence is a more permanent concept than residence and is the country in which the taxpayer is habitually resident, while domicile is the country which a taxpayer considers to be his permanent home, and once a particular domicile has been established it is generally very difficult to change it. Historically there has been a favourable tax regime for individuals who are resident, but not domiciled, in the UK, but due to the widespread perception of abuse of this regime by wealthy individuals who had been resident in the UK for many years, some changes were introduced in April 2008.

16.2. Residence – Statutory Definition

An individual is resident in the UK:

- if he is present in the UK for at least 183 days in the tax year, excluding the days of arrival and departure. Days spent in the UK due to circumstances beyond his control are not ignored for the purpose of this rule;
- if he is in the UK with a view or intent of establishing residence here;
- if he makes regular and substantial visits to the UK. This is generally interpreted to be visits totalling an average of more than 91 days in a tax year (excluding periods spent in the UK due to circumstances beyond his control, such as illness) over a period of four years;
- where a taxpayer has previously been ordinarily resident in the UK, he will be treated as resident in the UK if he is present in the UK at any time during a tax year.

By statute, a taxpayer's residence status is determined for a whole tax year; a tax year cannot generally be apportioned between periods of residence and non-residence. It should also be noted that different countries use different criteria to determine residence status, and it is therefore possible for a taxpayer to be resident in two or more countries at any particular time. Where this is the case, a taxpayer's country of residence will normally be determined by the relevant double taxation agreement (see 16.11).

16.3. Ordinary Residence

There is no statutory definition of ordinary residence, but the term 'ordinary' is given its normal definition and a taxpayer is ordinarily resident in the UK if he is habitually resident here. It is therefore possible to be resident in the UK, but not ordinarily resident or vice versa. A taxpayer will generally be considered to be ordinarily resident in the UK once he has been resident in the UK for three consecutive tax years, and will generally be considered to cease being ordinarily resident after being non-resident in the UK for three consecutive tax years.

As with a taxpayer's residence status, his ordinary residence status is determined for a whole tax year and a tax year cannot generally be split between periods of being ordinarily resident and being not ordinarily resident in the UK.

16.4. HM Revenue & Customs' Practice

HM Revenue & Customs will, by concession, permit a tax year to be apportioned between periods of residence and non-residence under certain circumstances. Where a taxpayer arrives in the UK with the intention of remaining in the UK for at least two years, he will be considered to be resident from the date of arrival. If a taxpayer arrives in the UK with the intention of remaining in the UK for at least three years, he will also be considered to be ordinarily resident in the UK from the date of arrival. If he owns accommodation in the UK on arrival, or purchases or leases accommodation in the UK in the tax year in which he arrives he will similarly be treated as being resident and ordinarily resident from the date of arrival.

In the year of departure from the UK in order to take up permanent residence abroad, or live abroad for at least three years, the taxpayer will cease to be resident and ordinarily resident from the day after the date of departure. The taxpayer must demonstrate evidence of this intention, for example by selling his residence in the UK and purchasing a new residence abroad. Where a taxpayer acquires property abroad, but retains property in the UK for his use, this will not necessarily preclude him from being treated as non-resident, if the reason for doing so is consistent with his aim of living abroad permanently.

Where a taxpayer goes abroad for the purpose of taking up employment and is abroad for a complete tax year, he will be treated as being not resident and not ordinarily resident from the day after his departure to the day before his return, provided that visits to the UK during this period do not exceed an average of 91 days per tax year and 183 days in any one tax year. The absence will start on the day after the taxpayer actually leaves the country rather than the day after the contract starts. The taxpayer's spouse will also be treated as being not resident and not ordinarily resident during this period if he or she accompanies the taxpayer.

The residence status of a married couple is determined independently and it is possible for one spouse to be resident and/or ordinarily resident during a tax year, and the other spouse to be not resident and/or not ordinarily resident.

16.5. Domicile

Domicile is a term of general law and an individual's place of domicile will be in the country which he considers to be his permanent home. This implies a much greater degree of permanence than being ordinarily resident and it is quite possible for a taxpayer born in, say, Australia to be a long-term resident of the UK, but to remain domiciled in Australia.

At birth an individual acquires a domicile of origin. This is not necessarily the country in which he is born, but will be the country of domicile of his father if his parents are married or the country of domicile of his mother if they are not. From the age of 16, it is possible to acquire a domicile of choice. Apart from the situation where an individual is born and brought up in the UK, but has a domicile of origin in, for example, France due to having a French father, it is extremely difficult to abandon a domicile of origin. It is necessary to show that he has abandoned all ties with his country of origin and now considers his country of residence to be his new permanent home.

Until 1 January 1974 a married woman acquired the domicile of her husband on marriage, but for marriages after that date the domiciles of a husband and wife are determined independently.

For the purpose of inheritance tax only a taxpayer can be deemed to be domiciled in the UK, even he is not domiciled here under general law. A taxpayer is deemed to be domiciled in the UK if he:
* has been resident in the UK for at least 17 of the previous 20 tax years; or
* has been domiciled in the UK at any time in the previous three years. If a taxpayer were to emigrate, severing all ties with the UK, he would remain domiciled in the UK for the purpose of inheritance tax for three years after the date of departure notwithstanding the position in general law.

16.6. Remittance Basis

Income is generally taxed on the arising basis, i.e. it is taxed in the tax year that it arises, but in certain circumstances income is taxed on the remittance basis, i.e. it is taxed in the tax year in which the income is remitted to the UK. The remittance basis has historically applied to individuals who are either not ordinarily resident or not domiciled in the UK, but due to widespread publicity about very wealthy individuals in the UK who used their non-domiciliary status to avoid paying UK on large amounts of income, the remittance basis rules were amended to restrict the use of this basis in April 2008. These rules only apply to non-domiciliaries who have been resident in the UK for at least seven of the previous nine tax years. Under the new rules non-domiciliaries must make a claim to use the remittance basis on their tax return, unless their foreign income in below a *de minimis* limit of £2,000. If they elect to use the remittance basis, they must pay a remittance basis charge of £30,000. The tax paid by non-domiciliaries will therefore be the higher of £30,000 and the tax on the income actually remitted to the UK during the tax year. A taxpayer who claims the remittance (but not a taxpayer who is automatically entitled to use the remittance basis) is not entitled to claim any personal allowances or tax reducers. Whilst the UK tax regime is still favourable to non-domiciliaries, whose foreign income in many cases runs into millions of pounds, the new rules at least ensure that these individuals pay some tax in the UK. It had been suggested that the remittance basis be abolished, but this dropped due to concern that the non-domiciliaries would leave the country if they had to pay UK tax on their foreign income.

16.7. Unremittable Income

Where income arising in a territory is taxable on an arising basis and cannot be remitted to the UK due to:
- the laws of the country in which the income arose;
- the executive action of its government; or
- the impossibility of obtaining currency which could be remitted to the UK;

and the taxpayer has not realised the income outside the territory in sterling or another currency which may be remitted to the UK a claim may be made for such income not to be taxed.

16.8. Personal Allowances

The following non-residents may claim personal allowances, provided that they have not made a claim to be taxed on the remittance basis. These include both allowances which are deducted from total income and tax reducers:

- citizens of the Commonwealth or European Economic Area (EU plus Switzerland, Liechtenstein, Norway and Iceland);
- residents of the Isle of Man and the Channel Islands;
- current or former Crown Servants and their widows or widowers;
- former residents of the UK who have moved abroad for health reasons; or
- missionaries.

Where a taxpayer is resident in the UK for only part of the year, i.e. the split year treatment applies, full personal allowances are available.

16.9. Transfer of Assets Abroad

There are anti-avoidance provisions to prevent a person who is ordinarily resident in the UK transferring an asset abroad, so that income from that asset is received by a person who is either resident or domiciled outside the UK. The income arising in such circumstances would normally be exempt, but where the transferor, or another person who is ordinarily resident in the UK, has the ability to enjoy the income or receives a capital sum in connection with the asset, the income is assessable on the transferor. A typical strategy which this legislation aims to counteract is the transfer of an asset into a non-resident trust where the transferor is one of the beneficiaries.

These provisions will not apply if it can be shown that the transfer was undertaken for genuine commercial reasons and that tax avoidance was not one of the motives.

16.10. Double Tax Relief

16.10.1.Introduction

Where a taxpayer is resident in the UK, but derives income from another country, or is resident in another country and has income derived from the UK, it is likely that he will be subject to tax in both the UK and the other country, but there are provisions to prevent, or at least to mitigate, the effect of double taxation. These are generally through double tax agreements which have been negotiated between the UK and most foreign countries, the provisions of which take precedence over domestic UK tax law. Statute provides for unilateral relief if there is no double tax agreement with the particular country, or a particular situation is not covered by a double tax agreement.

If double tax relief cannot be obtained in the tax year that the income is taxable, for example if there is no taxable income in the state of residence, relief is lost; there is no carry forward or carry back of overseas tax. It is, therefore, important to consider the effect of loss relief claims on double tax relief.

Where there is a change in the amount of overseas tax suffered on income, e.g. the amount has not been finalised at the date of making the UK tax return, and the amount of double tax relief claimed is later found to be excessive, the taxpayer must notify HM Revenue & Customs.

16.10.2.Unilateral Credit Relief

Where double tax relief is not available under the terms of a double tax agreement, unilateral relief is available unless the agreement expressly excludes double tax relief. Relief is generally given by giving credit for the overseas tax suffered on the income against the UK tax liability. Credit is given up to a maximum of the lower of:

• the overseas tax suffered; and
• the UK tax payable on the income.

Credit relief is ignored when calculating the income available for tax reducers.

The effect of unilateral relief is that the taxpayer will suffer the higher of the UK tax and the overseas tax on the income. The overseas income is treated as the top slice of the taxpayer's income, and, where there is more than one source of overseas income, the top slice will be the overseas income which has suffered overseas tax at the highest rate.

16.10.3. Expense Relief

Where there is no advantage in claiming credit relief, for example because of loss relief claims, it is possible to claim expense relief. In this case only the net income after overseas tax is brought into the tax computation.

16.11. Double Tax Agreements

16.11.1.Scope of Double Tax Agreements

In the vast majority of cases double tax relief will be available under the terms of the double tax agreement between the UK and the relevant overseas territory. Since these agreements are all negotiated individually between the UK and the overseas territory, and the domestic tax regime in the overseas territory will be different in each case, the detailed provisions of each treaty will vary. Any question of treaty relief can therefore only be resolved by reference to the relevant treaty. Nevertheless, they will all cover broadly the same areas and there are many points of similarity between the great majority of treaties. In respect of a particular type of income the treaty will generally provide that:

• it will be taxed in the country of residence of the taxpayer; or

- it will be taxed in the source country; or
- a reduced rate of tax will be applied in both countries.

Relief may be given for any foreign taxes specified in an agreement. HM Revenue & Customs have published a list of admissible and inadmissible foreign taxes.

Where a country gives a taxpayer a tax holiday as an incentive to promote industrial, commercial, scientific educational or other development, any tax spared is treated as tax payable and a creditable tax for the purpose of double taxation relief in order not to lose the benefit of this incentive. This relief is only available under a double taxation treaty, not under the provisions for unilateral relief.

HM Revenue & Customs' obligation of secrecy does not prevent the disclosure of information necessary for giving double tax relief to the tax authorities of other countries and many double tax treaties contain provisions for the exchange of information. Where a taxpayer claims that he is not being taxed in accordance with a double tax treaty, either in the UK or the foreign territory, and HM Revenue & Customs believe that he has a justifiable case, HMRC may resolve the issue either unilaterally or by agreement with the foreign tax authority, notwithstanding any statutory provisions to the contrary.

16.11.2.Model Double Tax Treaty

The Organisation for Economic Co-operation and Development (OECD) has published a model treaty and most of the double tax agreements concluded by the UK will broadly follow this model. The model treaty covers the following main areas.

Residence

Since all territories will have their own rules for determining residence it is possible for a taxpayer to be resident in two or more territories in any tax year (the fact that other territories do not have a tax year ending on the distinctly eccentric date of 5 April further complicates the matter). A treaty will therefore include 'tie-breakers' in such cases to determine the issue.

Business Profits

Business profits will be taxable in the taxpayer's country of residence, unless the business has a permanent establishment in the other country, such as a branch or agency. Where a business carries on a business in another territory through a permanent establishment, it is possible to manipulate the profits of that establishment for tax purposes (and also of the main business) by transferring goods between the two either at over-value or at under-value. Where this occurs an adjustment will be made so that the profits attributed to a business will be those which would have arisen if such transactions had taken place on an arm's length basis.

Associated Enterprises/Transfer Pricing

Where an enterprise of one country controls an enterprise in the other country, or enterprises in the two countries are under common control, and transactions or financial arrangements between the two are not on an arm's length basis, a similar adjustment will be made.

Dividends

The principal taxing rights for dividends lie with the territory of residence of the taxpayer, but the source territory may also charge tax on the dividend at a rate not exceeding 15%.

Interest

The principal taxing rights for interest lie with the territory of residence of the taxpayer, but the source territory may also charge tax at a rate not exceeding 10%.

Royalties

Royalties are taxable in the territory of residence of the taxpayer.

Capital Gains

Gains arising on the sale of immovable property are taxed in the territory in which the property is situated. Gains arising on the sale of movable property are taxed in the territory in which the taxpayer is resident.

Wages, Salaries and Other Remuneration

Wages and salaries will be taxable in the territory in which the taxpayer is resident, unless the employment is exercised in an overseas territory.

Pensions

Pensions are in general only taxable in the territory in which the taxpayer is resident.

Capital Taxation

This covers taxes such as inheritance tax or a wealth tax. Immovable property situated in an overseas territory, or movable property which forms part of a permanent establishment situated in the overseas territory, may be taxed in the overseas territory. Other property will be taxed in the territory in which the taxpayer is resident.

Methods of Eliminating Double Taxation

States may either exempt the overseas income from tax or give credit for overseas tax suffered against tax charged in that state, i.e. by deducting the overseas tax paid from the tax payable in the state of residence. The UK uses the latter method and foreign tax which may be deducted is the lower of the overseas tax payable on the overseas income and the UK tax attributable to that income.

Non-discrimination

A state may not treat non-residents or non-nationals less favourably than residents or nationals of that state.

Chapter 17. Pensions

17.1. Introduction

A new pensions regime was introduced by the Finance Act 2004 Part 4, which came into force on 6 April 2006 (A-Day). The main features of the new regime are:

1. each taxpayer is entitled to a single lifetime allowance on the amount of pension savings which qualify for tax relief. This limit was set at £1,650,000 in 2008/09, rising to £1,750,000 in 2009/10 and £1,800,000 in 2010/11. Thereafter the limit will be reviewed every five years. Benefits in excess of the limit taken in the form of pensions are taxed at 25%, or 55% if they are taken as a lump sum;

2. pension rights accrued at 6 April 2006 are protected by the new regime;

3. the ability to enjoy tax relief in respect of contributions made (in the case of a defined contribution pension scheme) or pensions accrued (in respect of a defined benefit scheme) in any particular year by or on behalf of an individual is limited to an individual's Annual Allowance. For the tax year 2008/2009, the Annual Allowance was £235,000, rising to £245,000 in 2009/10 and £255,000 in 2010/11. Thereafter the limit will be reviewed every five years *(FA 2004 ss.227 & 228)*. Contributions in excess of the annual limit are taxed at 40%. It should, however, be noted that an individual may only obtain tax relief in respect of his or her own contributions (to a registered defined contribution scheme) insofar as they do not exceed the greater of £3,600 per annum or 100% of their relevant UK earnings (up to the Annual Allowance) that are subject to income tax for the tax year in question. If an individual has no relevant UK earnings, he or she may still qualify for tax relief on contributions to a registered pension scheme up to £3,600 per annum (see chapter 17.2 below);

4. pension funds may offer members a tax-free lump sum of up to 25% of the value of the pension fund;

5. members of registered pension schemes may draw retirement benefits whilst they are still working, if the rules of the scheme permit. At present, (other than in cases of ill-health) pensions may not be taken before the age of 50. The minimum retirement age will be raised from 50 to 55 on 6 April 2010.

17.2. Scope of Regime

Pension schemes qualifying for relief under the regime are called *registered pension schemes*. A registered pension scheme is a scheme registered with HM Revenue & Customs providing for benefits to be paid to members on death, retirement, the onset of serious ill-health or incapacity, the attainment of a given age or in similar circumstances.

An employer or employers may establish a pension scheme to provide benefits to all employees of that or those employer(s) or any other employer, regardless of whether it may also provide benefits to other persons. These pension schemes are called *occupational pension schemes*. An employer whose employees may benefit from an occupational pension scheme is termed a *sponsoring employer*. An occupational pension scheme may have more than one employer "participating" in it.

The pension scheme may be a *money purchase arrangement*, a *defined benefit arrangement* or a *hybrid arrangement*, containing a mixture of money purchase and defined benefit arrangements. Under a money purchase scheme (sometimes referred to as a "defined contribution scheme"), contributions are paid into the scheme by and/or on behalf of a member, invested on behalf of that member, and the resulting "pensions pot" then used to fund the benefits when they come into payment. In contrast, under a defined benefit arrangement, a member's pension will be calculated by reference to a formula (typically 1/60 of the member's "final pensionable salary" for each year of pensionable service) and thus the member's pensions entitlement is not (directly) dependent upon the contribution rate(s) and/or investment return earned by the contributions.

Personal pension schemes (and stakeholder pension schemes) are arrangements made between individuals and the pension provider, who will usually be an insurance company or similar organisation. Employers may make contributions to such schemes, but play no role in administering them. Employers may use such schemes to provide a 'group personal pension scheme' for their employees, but this is, in fact, just a collection of individual personal pension schemes, usually provided by the same provider. Money invested in personal pension schemes is invested by the provider and, upon retirement, the balance in the fund is used to purchase an annuity (and possibly a tax-free lump sum). The value of the pension will therefore depend on the stock market at the date of retirement.

Stakeholder pension schemes are a special type of personal pension scheme. They are designed to encourage individuals to save for their retirement and to have a low cost and simple charging structure; providers of stakeholder pension schemes are not permitted to levy annual charges exceeding 1% of the accumulated fund (1.5% for the first ten years) or to penalise members for varying their pension contributions or transferring accumulated money purchase balances in or out of the scheme. Employers (unless exempt from the stakeholder requirements) are obliged to provide details of the schemes to their employees and allow any employee who wishes to do so to contribute to such schemes through payroll deductions, but they are not obliged to contribute to the schemes themselves, although they may do so if they wish.

17.3. Payments by Registered Pension Schemes

A registered pension scheme may only make the following types of payments (known as "authorised member payments") to persons who are, or who have been, members:

1. pension payments or pension death benefits. These include annuities and income withdrawals;
2. lump sums payments or lump sum death benefits;
3. recognised transfers;
4. scheme administration member payments;
5. payments pursuant to a pension sharing order;
6. payments prescribed by regulations made by HM Revenue & Customs.

No pension payment may be made until the member reaches the normal minimum pension age (age 50 before 6 April 2010; age 55 thereafter), unless the ill-health condition is met, which requires that:

(a) the scheme administrator has received evidence from a registered medical practitioner that the member is (and will continue to be) incapable of carrying on the member's occupation because of physical or mental impairment, and

(b) the member has in fact ceased to carry on the member's occupation.

If the member dies within 10 years of becoming entitled to a pension, an annuity or alternatively secured pension may continue to be made to any other person until the end of the 10-year period, but no other payment may be made after the member's death.

17.4. Contributions

17.4.1. Members' Contributions

A member of a registered pension scheme may claim tax relief on relievable pension contributions if the member has earnings from relevant UK earnings (income from employment or self-employment) chargeable to UK income tax during the tax year or is resident in the UK at some time in the tax.

A member is entitled to relief on the greater of contributions on 100% of their relevant UK earnings (subject to the Annual Allowance), or on £3,600. Tax relief for contributions is given at source at the basic rate unless the pension scheme is permitted to operate a net pay arrangement.

17.4.2. Employers' Contributions

Employers may claim relief on contributions to registered pension schemes on behalf of their employees. Relief may be claimed by deduction from trading profits or as an expense of management or as an expense of insurance companies. Employers' contributions are not taxable on members as benefits in kind.

Where an employer's contribution in the current chargeable period is more than 210% of the contribution in the preceding chargeable period, relief for the excess contribution, provided that it is at least £500,000, may be spread over the current and immediately following periods, depending on the amount of the excess contribution.

17.4.3. HM Revenue & Customs Contributions

Where an employee holds an appropriate personal pension scheme and has contracted out of the State Second Pension, HM Revenue & Customs is required to make payments to the employee's registered pension scheme.

17.5. Unauthorised Payments Charge

Any payments made by a registered pension scheme other than those authorised by FA 2004 Pt 4 are subject to a tax charge of 40%. This charge applies to payments made to persons who are, or who have been, members or to a sponsoring employer. The person liable to the charge is the member or sponsoring employer to whom the payment is made. Where the payment represents 25% or more of the fund value at the date of the payment FA 2004 s.209 imposes an additional surcharge of 15%, bringing the total charge to 55% of the payment.

17.6. Special Annual Allowance Charge

Finance Act 2009 Sch.35 has introduced an income tax charge of 20% on pension contributions and benefits above a limit of £20,000 accruing to individuals with a relevant income in excess of £150,000. It does not apply to the normal pattern of pension contributions, but only where individuals change their pattern of saving. This measure has been introduced in anticipation of the restriction of tax relief on pension contributions to the basic rate with effect from 6 April 2011 in order to forestall high income individuals from increasing their contributions before the restriction comes into force.

Chapter 18.　　Anti-avoidance

18.1.　Introduction

Traditionally, the difference between tax avoidance and tax evasion has been that tax avoidance involves the taxpayer using the tax rules to his best advantage to minimise his tax liability, whilst tax evasion involves dishonesty where the taxpayer either deliberately falsifies returns, and possibly also supporting documentation, or conceals information which HM Revenue & Customs have a right to know. A common example of the latter is where a taxpayer runs a business without informing HMRC. Tax avoidance is therefore legal, whilst tax evasion is illegal and the only penalty to a taxpayer for a failed tax avoidance scheme, provided that they have been honest with HMRC, is that they do not get the tax advantage they were seeking. For the government and HMRC this has caused a problem because a cat-and-mouse game has developed between them and taxpayers and their advisors where tax advisors devise tax avoidance schemes to reduce their clients' tax liabilities. HMRC's only recourses have been first to challenge the scheme through the courts and, if the challenge fails, to reactively enact specific anti-avoidance legislation to prevent other taxpayers taking advantage of the same scheme. Tax advisors will then try to devise ways of circumventing the new anti-avoidance legislation. This process has been a contributory factor in the increasing complexity of the UK tax system.

HMRC and the government have changed their strategy towards tax avoidance to try to cut down the use of such schemes. In public debate, if not in law, tax avoidance has been divided into 'acceptable' and 'unacceptable' tax avoidance by HMRC, although taxpayers and tax advisors may not agree with this distinction. Acceptable tax avoidance, or tax planning, involves the use of provisions expressly enacted to enable taxpayers to reduce their tax liabilities. An example of such tax avoidance might be the use of Individual Savings Accounts (ISAs), which were set up to encourage taxpayers to save by allowing them to do so tax-free, subject to limits. Unacceptable tax avoidance involves the use of artificial transactions or structures to reduce a tax liability. For example, groups of companies may have a complex structure which diverts taxable profits to low-tax regimes such as the Cayman Islands, or the Swiss canton of Zug in a well-publicised case involving Tesco plc, even if no commercial activity takes place there. In order to counteract the use of unacceptable tax avoidance more effectively the use of a General Anti-avoidance Rule has often been suggested. Such a rule has never been introduced in the UK. However, the Finance Act 2009 has introduced more targeted anti-avoidance rules and the Finance Acts 2004 and 2006 introduced a requirement to give HMRC advance notice of certain tax avoidance schemes.

18.2.   General and Targeted Anti-avoidance Rules

A General Anti-avoidance Rule (GAAR) would give HMRC wide discretion to disallow tax avoidance schemes without giving a specific reason, if it feels that they are artificial or abusive. The GAAR has also been termed a General Anti-avoidance Principle (abbreviated GANTIP to avoid confusion with accounting GAAP). Such a rule has never been introduced in the UK, although Australia introduced a GAAR a number of years ago. It is, therefore, unclear what rights a taxpayer might have to appeal against a decision of HMRC. If the courts showed willingness to intervene, their decisions would create precedents about when a GAAR might be invoked which could undermine the purpose of such a rule. If courts refused to intervene, such a rule might be seen as an unacceptable transfer of power to HMRC. For this reason a GAAR might be most effective if it is not invoked, but is simply used as a deterrent to prevent the schemes being devised in the first place.

An alternative to a GAAR is a targeted anti-avoidance rules (TAAR), which give HMRC the power to disallow schemes in specific areas. The Finance Act 2009 has introduced a TAAR to counteract tax planning arrangements which use the corporation tax regime relating to the hedging of currency risk in an asymmetric manner, i.e. the losses would be tax-deductible, but the gains not taxable. This is the first time that such a rule has been introduced, and it is still unclear how this rule might operate in practice.

18.3.   Transfer Pricing

Transfer pricing is a means by which companies in a group can shift profits between different companies and between different tax jurisdictions. If a UK company manufactures goods and wishes to transfer them to an overseas subsidiary for sale, the price at which, and the terms under which, the goods are transferred need not be the same as those which would have been negotiated if the transfer had been an arm's-length transaction Tax considerations may therefore determine the transfer price. If the overseas tax rate is lower than in the UK, a transfer price close to cost price will ensure that most of the group profit will arise in the overseas subsidiary, whilst, if the overseas tax rate is higher than in the UK, a transfer price close to selling price will ensure that most of the group profit will arise in the UK.

There is therefore anti-avoidance legislation to prevent the artificial shifting of profits into low-tax jurisdictions. There is a general provision which assumes that for tax purposes transactions between connected parties take place on arm's-length terms, and that, if the terms are different from these, an appropriate adjustment is made. There is also more specific legislation, for example provisions counteracting *thin capitalisation*, whereby an overseas subsidiary is set up with minimal share capital and is financed almost entirely by an inter-company loan, thereby creating a gearing ratio far excess of what would normally be commercially acceptable. Interest on the loan would normally be tax deductible, thus allowing the parent company to transfer profits out of the subsidiary, whereas a dividend is paid out of taxed profits. The anti-avoidance legislation recharacterises interest on the part of the loan in excess of what would be advanced on arm's-length terms as a dividend.

18.4. Disclosure of Tax Avoidance Schemes

18.4.1. Notifiable Schemes

Tax advisors are required to disclose to HM Revenue & Customs 'notifiable arrangements', i.e. principally, arrangements involving certain financial or employment products from which a user of arrangements might be expected to obtain a tax advantage as a main benefit. The term 'arrangements' is defined as covering 'any scheme, transaction or series of transactions' and is not restricted to arrangements which are actually implemented. Regulations published in August 2004 have made it clear that these provisions only apply in restricted circumstances and do not apply to include normal tax advice.

Arrangements are only notifiable if a tax advantage in the arrangements arises 'to a significant degree' from a financial product and if they fail all of the following tests:

Premium Fee Test
This test is failed if the promoter, or a person connected with him, has, or would be able to, obtain a premium rate fee.

Confidentiality Test
The confidentiality test is failed if a promoter might reasonably wish to keep the tax avoidance element confidential. The promoter's duty of confidentiality to his client and any other legal obligations are ignored, and the test looks at whether a promoter may wish to keep the arrangement confidential in order to preserve a competitive advantage; therefore this test is not failed if the tax avoidance element is well-known to tax advisers.

Off-Market Test
Where a promoter is a party to the financial product, this test is failed if the terms are significantly different from those which could be obtained on the open market.

Arrangements involving employment products are notifiable if they involve products which might be expected to give a reduction in, or a deferment of, the tax liability of an employee and involve one or more of the following:

- securities, interests in securities, securities options or any right derived from securities;
- payments to trustees and intermediaries; or
- loans.

From 1 August 2005, the disclosure regime was extended to arrangements involving high value commercial property (£5 million or more) where avoidance of SDLT was a main, or one of the main, benefits expected to arise from the transaction. The premium fee and confidentiality filters do not apply to SDLT arrangements.

18.4.2. Promoters
The details must be notified by a 'promoter', i.e. any person who conducts a relevant business who is to any extent responsible for the design, organisation or management of the arrangements or who makes the arrangements available for implementation by others. A relevant business is one which involves the provision of services related to taxation or banking services. Employees and office-holders are not treated as promoters.

A person makes a proposal 'available for implementation by other persons' as opposing to being involved in the design if, for example, he is responsible for the marketing and distribution of the arrangements or the introduction of the client and the person making the arrangements. Being a designer of a proposal involves, for example, confirming that the arrangements are effective and identifying flaws and advising of minor changes.

18.4.3. Procedure for Notifying Arrangements
The promoter must inform HMRC of such details as may be prescribed in regulations issued by the Treasury within five days from the earlier of the date that he makes a proposal available for implementation or becomes aware of any transaction forming part of the arrangements taking place.

HM Revenue & Customs may allocate the arrangements a reference number within 30 days of being notified. This does not mean that HMRC consider the arrangements might, in law, result in a person obtaining a tax advantage i.e. that they are likely to work, but the system should enable HMRC to keep track of arrangements notified and current avoidance schemes. A promoter must notify the client of the reference number within 30 days of becoming aware of any transaction forming part of the arrangements or of HMRC's notifying the number to the promoter, if later. Any party to the notifiable arrangements must notify HMRC of any reference number which has been notified to him by a promoter, and of the time when he obtains, or expects to obtain a tax advantage. HMRC will, therefore, know precisely which parties are involved in any notifiable arrangements. It also ensures that tax payers get streated consistently as all users of the same tax avoidance scheme are reviewed by the same HMRC team. HMRC do not issue a reference number in relation to SDLT arrangements.

Information which is covered by legal privilege need not be disclosed. Accordingly, where advice in relation to arrangements is given by a solicitor or barrister and is privileged, the obligation to disclose shifts from promoter to user of the arrangements (the client).

18.4.4. Penalties

The penalty for a failure by a promoter to notify HM Revenue & Customs of notifiable arrangements is a fine of up to £5,000, plus up to £600 per day after the imposition of the initial penalty whilst the failure persists.

The penalty for failing to notify HM Revenue & Customs of the scheme number provided to a user of arrangements by a promoter is:

* £100 for the first failure;
* £500 for the second failure;
* £500 for a third and subsequent failure.

These penalties will be imposed in all cases of non-compliance unless there is a reasonable excuse or the taxpayer or advisor has made a reasonable judgement as to whether he is obliged to make a disclosure.

Index

INTRODUCTION TO THE UK TAX SYSTEM

INTRODUCTION TO THE UK TAX SYSTEM